Values Your Lives

Lives

The way Jesus wants us to think and act

British Library Cataloguing in Publication Data.
A catalogue record for this book is available from
the British Library.

ISBN 978-1-78665-030-6

Unless where otherwise indicated, Scripture
quotations in this book are taken from the
English Standard Version (Anglicised).

Other translations used:
King James (Authorised) Version (KJV)
New International Version (NIV)
The Clear Word
J. B. Phillips

All emphases are the author's.

Designed by David Bell.
Cover design by David Bell.
Printed in Serbia.

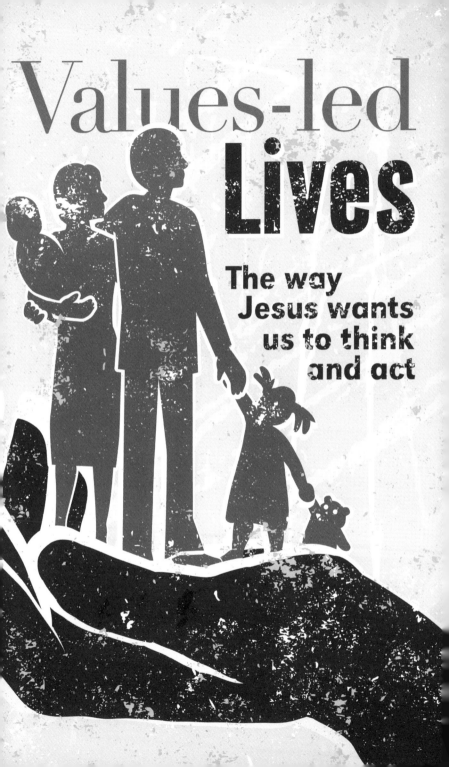

Values-led
Lives

The way Jesus wants us to think and act

Contents

Preface

This book about living the values-led life has grown out of a number of concerns and hopes.

- A sampling of these concerns include . . .
- The haemorrhaging of our youth from the church
- Loss of our PKs (preacher's kids)
- Disappearance of white young people
- And more recently the numbers of black young people leaving the church

It is based on the experience of visiting churches that seem at times to be oppressive; where the slogans and posters used appear to express a distant, legal and formal god rather than the gracious God we, in theory, believe in.

It is written out of concern for those sermons and services that should have carried the disclaimer: For members only!

It is written out of concern for the number of people who have said that they cannot bring their friends to their church.

It is written out of concern for the pastors, elders, deaconesses and deacons who don't seem to understand how to embed the core values of the Kingdom into the culture of their churches.

It is written to give hope to those faithful members who continue to attend but long for a better church.

It is written in the hope that our revival and reformation services will lead not only to individual spirituality, but more importantly (in my opinion) to corporate spirituality.

It is written in the belief that the Adventist Church in the UK, USA and elsewhere is at a point when we are multicultural enough both to recognise that our problems and conflicts are not so much racist as cultural, and that we can address these problems with our common humanity and clear Kingdom values.

It is written in the belief that the present generation of young pastors, both black and white, are able to address our differences with new eyes: that recognise that we need to address the matter of the corporate culture of our churches in order to both keep our young people and reach the people around us.

It is written in the recognition that both church and secular people expect values that 'exceed' in our churches. (See Matthew 5:20, KJV.)

How to use this book
This book is not to be read as a novel. It is more suitable for use as a map – and that depends on just where you are on the journey of being 'values-led'. My start into the topic is slow, simply because I have found that there are some people and congregations who look blankly at me when I begin talking about the importance of values. I can see them searching through their minds for a text that says, 'Thou shalt be values-led.' And, not finding the verse, they wonder

if I am attempting to introduce some new, unbiblical 'light'. This is why I like Tom Wright's rewording of the word *values* as 'virtues' in his book, *Virtue Reborn*. In my presentations I often use the words 'virtue' and 'principle' in place of the word 'value' to lessen that fear of this unfamiliar word. I would advise a similar slow approach if you decide to become a values-led person or want to guide your organisation in that direction.

Once the importance of values is seen and the decision is made to adopt a values-led approach to life, the middle sections of the book (roughly chapters 14 to 24) become important. There are examples of value statements and the 'how to' information that you will need to implement them.

The last section of the book contains some reflections about being values-led from a scriptural perspective. Reading, particularly of the gospels, through values spectacles has given me a whole new insight into things. In each story of Jesus I find myself amazed as I watch Him act and speak from a value-embedded character. I understand so much more now about how a virtue or principle or value differs from an application of that value. I see God's core value of grace in His dealings with people much more clearly now and I look forward to continuing that journey as I explore why He acted the way He did, particularly in the Old Testament. For me this journey began in my younger years with the reading of Alden Thompson's book, *Who's Afraid of the Old Testament God?*

So you might want to read the last section of this book first and the middle section last – it all depends where you are on the journey.

Chapter 1

Introduction: becoming values-led – my journey

S ome years ago I had the privilege of completing an MA in leadership, and as part of the course we were invited to create a personal value statement. At the time I did not realise the significance of what I was about to do. I thought I would simply list some Christian virtues that I hold as biblical and that conformed to the professional standards of being a Seventh-day Adventist pastor. I expected that they would act as a sort of fence within which I could perform my role as a pastor.

It took me six months of struggling to complete this task. It involved questioning my motives, journalling about how I had responded to various situations, and much prayer. There were also times when I offered strong resistance to the Spirit, who was calling me to honesty and accountability. Maybe the most powerful and ongoing part of this process was my effort to discern and contemplate with awe the personal values that inspired Jesus' life and actions. This helped me see how far I fell short of being like Jesus – God's living Value Statement. All this resulted in several re-rankings of my stated values, and in some cases certain of those values were deleted while new ones were added.

Over the years I've come to realise that a value statement

is about you – who you are at your inner core. It is a statement of *who you are* and not a statement of **what** you want to achieve (vision-goals), or of **how** to achieve your vision (strategy). It is a statement of who you want to be and of who God wants you to be. In the end it is a statement of being, or at least a statement about the being I want to be.

One of our problems is that we tend to define ourselves by the expectations of our role or job, or by the expectations of our employers, our parents or our church. But those expectations are not necessarily who we are. I can fulfil all the outward expectations and get the job done, but be another person inside. Being a butcher, a baker or a candlestick maker, or even a minister, an elder or a long-time Adventist, doesn't necessarily make me a nice person. What I do does not define me. Neither, necessarily, do my doctrinal beliefs. Who I am is my inner core values. And it is out of these, not any outward expectations, that what I do should flow. Values have to do with first cleaning the 'inside of the cup and the plate, that the outside also may be clean' (Matt. 23:26).

One can ask the question, 'What or who is God?' and the reply can include all the 'omnis' one can think of, but what really matters in the end is what He is on the inside – His character or nature. I would guess that one day on the New Earth, were the saved suddenly to discover that God is actually a bully and tyrant, they might vote for another rebellion. The core issue of the great controversy is not about finding fault with His abilities or His role – it is about His character and the values He holds at the core of His being.

The significance of this struck me when I was working in Egypt with my value statement completed – or, more accurately, completed up to that stage. In actual fact it keeps growing as my understanding of the character of God increases. I titled the page 'Llew's Constitution', printed it off in large print and placed it centrally on my desk. It was in large print so that I could read it at a glance, but also because I wanted all who interacted with me to know that this is what they should expect of me. And if I did not meet those values they should call me to be accountable to them. Value statements have a healthy way of moving one's judgemental eye away from one's neighbour to one's self.

In this very different Middle Eastern culture my 'constitution' was to prove very important. I was often confronted by behaviours and decisions that I wasn't sure how to relate to. When I was not sure how to act I would look to my value statement, say an inner prayer, and then choose to act in harmony with my chosen values. I was amazed at how those values stood me in good stead in the midst of a culture that was very different from that which I was used to. They became not only a compass to guide my behaviour, but also a guide to recognising how a legitimate value needed to be subjected in some situations to a higher value.

One specific experience that helped me understand this was a church in Upper Egypt that had a wooden screen or wall that separated the men from the women. My immediate reaction was to work towards taking the wall down – it was not right to have this separation. Equality in church is a value. So on one of my visits there I asked the pastor for permission to conduct a verbal survey during the church service. With permission granted I asked for all the hands to go up of those who wanted the wall down. To my utter confusion, the men raised their hands in agreement but the women's hands stayed down! The two sides could not see each other so I surmised that they had misunderstood the pastor's translation of my question. He assured me that he had understood me and translated correctly. So, to make sure, I reversed the question by asking them to raise their hands if they wanted the wall to remain up. Every woman's hand went up and all the men's hands remained down.

I was nonplussed: so much so that I left the survey there, but later talked to the pastor and his wife about the vote. She told me that the women would like to have it down but feared the men's gaze, whereas the men would be 'happy' to have lovely ladies to look at in church. It became a matter of protecting the women. Immediately I recognised a higher value than equality. It was not about doing what was right – it was about doing what was good. It also highlighted the need for educating hearts towards Kingdom values.

Occasionally I would find myself acting contrary to my values, mainly because it didn't suit me or my wisdom at the time, and later, as I would journal on my decisions or actions, I always came to the conclusion that the values on my 'constitution' would have given me a truer guide to what my actions should have been. I had not followed the compass and essentially lost my way.

I also became aware that there was a conflict between my own heart, my inner core, and the values that I knew belonged to the Kingdom of Heaven. I began to realise that one of my primary tasks was to move the values off the page, for them not just to be moved into my head but to become embedded in my heart. The problem had to do with humanity's ability, as Isaiah 29:13 puts it, to 'honour me with their lips, while their hearts are far from me'. However, as I saw the beauty of Jesus' heart and values, I wanted more and more to make my heart like His: not a simple task! As a friend of mine told me recently, while seeking to make grace his core value he found himself tripping over an ungracious heart (his own). He told me, 'Llew – it is not easy! It is a struggle.' We then shared how wonderful it is that grace is His core value, and each time we fall short He lovingly picks us up, forgives us and empowers us to try again.

Another topic that arose out of my experience with a value statement was that of sanctification. I have always been very leery of perfectionism and perfect people. Frankly, I have seen some 'perfect' people that I wouldn't want to live in heaven with. As Mark Twain once put it, *'Heaven goes by favour; if it went by merit, you would stay out and your dog would go in.'*

Nevertheless, in my struggle with my value statement – a statement that continues to strangely evolve, becoming shorter in length yet wider in its implications – I began to think of the experience in terms of sanctification and soon saw sanctification not as *attainment but as aspiration*. It was an aspiration to relate to those around me with the values of the Kingdom of Heaven. It meant that the issue was no longer about me relating to God, but about me relating to others.

Then I began to see the church as the ideal place to grow in one's values. Sanctification was beginning to make sense to me if it occurs in community. In Galatians 4:19, it is Paul's wish that Christ be formed in that community. And this had to involve the discipline of the church becoming a values-led community. My reading also led me to see that most organisations that excel in what they do – be they secular or religious – have clear value statements. In such organisations they have a duty to hold each other accountable to the values they all signed up to aspire to, because the group's members are agreed about what they want to become. In this context criticism becomes a supportive and constructive discussion as together we work towards achieving the values that we aspire to. It becomes a privilege to excel, not a chore.

That's how I became interested in being values-led and began longing for values-led leadership and church communities.

Thus this little book of big values.

Chapter 2

Sweet – the scent of a values-led life

There was an advert some years ago for a perfume called 'Impulse'. A man is walking along a street and catches a whiff of an exquisite perfume. He turns, she has passed, he cannot see her face, but cannot resist the impulse to go after her with a flower and say thank you for making the world a sweeter place.

That is like meeting a Christian or a church that is values-led. You encounter them and, either immediately or as you walk away, you sense that you were in the presence of a fragrance that makes your life a better place to be.

The scent is indiscriminate; it is no respecter of persons. It reaches old and young alike, rich and poor, sinner and saint. It is seen in the gentle manner, in the sparkle in the eye, in the warming smile, in the listening ear, in the kind word, in the sympathetic touch. It welcomes you as a friend. It recognises your potential. It encourages your trust. It awakens hope. It replaces fear with a sense of expectation. It has a wisdom that reaches, not with the finger of judgement but with the outstretched arms of grace. The apostle James describes it as 'the wisdom that is from above [which] is first pure, then peaceable, gentle, and easy to be entreated, full of mercy and good fruits, without partiality, and without hypocrisy. And the fruit of righteousness is sown in peace of them that make peace.' James 3:17, 18 (KJV).

Being that fragrance, not just having it, results from a life in which the excelling values of the Kingdom of Heaven are consciously recognised and then embedded into the head, heart and hands of the disciples of Jesus. It makes one – quite unconsciously – a 'sweet savour . . . of life unto life'; – a 'living sacrifice'; 'acceptable, wellpleasing to God'. (Rom. 12:1; 2 Cor. 2:15, 16; Phil. 4:18, KJV.)

The Model of the values-led life is Jesus Christ. In Him the values of the Kingdom of Heaven were manifest in human flesh, for those values are His very character. The values are not a set of rules that He adheres to, they are Who He is – a Person. Ultimately they are the character of the Godhead and the subject of what we know as the central issue in the great controversy: what kind of Person is He?

The challenge for us as citizens of that Kingdom is to emit the scent of those values in our own lives and community. It is the contention of this book that that is unlikely to happen without a conscious, intentional, accountable, reflective, personal study of the values of the King, which are also those of His Kingdom.

It is the intention of this book to judge no one – that would contradict a manifest value of the Lord Jesus (Matt. 7:1; John 12:47) – but to inspire and help both our members and our organisations to become values-led.

In our journey we will share stories and their impact as odious or sweet. We will consider how and why people and organisations outside of ourselves are so often values-led. We will explore the beauty of the Kingdom and its values, and how they excel. We will ask what difference Kingdom values make and then we will explore how we as individuals, congregations, institutions and organisations can become values-led. Finally, we will spend some time gazing on the Person who personifies the values. Ultimately it is by beholding Him that we become changed.

The story is told of a drunk who goes each evening to a drop-in centre where part of the regime includes an evening talk. The drunk attends but doesn't follow too much – it is foreign to him and his mind is not too clear. There is an assistant there called Harry, who never fails to show the drunk gentle kindness and respect. One evening the drunk is trying to understand the preacher, but finding it all too much he eventually begins to complain and create a disturbance. Harry isn't there that evening and the other attendants try to subdue the drunk, who simply gets more agitated. The preacher gets involved and in desperation yells at the drunk, *'You need to be like Jesus!'* The drunk stops for a moment, looks at the preacher and says, *'I don't know Jesus. Is he like Harry? If he is then I would like to be like Him because I want to be like Harry!'* I don't know who that Harry was, but I would assess that Harry was a values-led person. If you had been there, above the alcohol and the smell of urine and cheap cigarettes, you would have smelt the scent of a values-led life.

Chapter 3

Love – the highest value

It isn't rocket science to work out the top-placed value. It is love – simply because 'God is love' (1 John 4:8). You could say, 'Love rules!'

But this also makes love the most difficult value to aspire to – it has a perfect model to emulate. All other values or fruits of the Spirit are relative. How much joy, peace, patience, kindness, goodness, faithfulness, gentleness and self-control are you supposed to have? Answer: as much as you can. But love that is any less than the perfect Father-type love isn't love.

The difficult part is understanding what love looks like.

We glibly read that God 'so loved the world'. But does that include the drug pushers, the alcoholics, the homeless, the gays, the transgenders, the cross-dressers, the child abusers, the terrorists, the zealots, the prostitutes, the tax collectors and the detestable sinners? *Strong's Concordance*, in its definition of the Bible word 'sinners', provides associated words to help the reader grasp its meaning. It includes words like *depraved* and *detestable*. The revulsion that can arise within us towards those whom we might class as 'detestable sinners' could influence how we define and understand the love that is to be valued. Passages such as

Psalm 139:21-22 may give a twist to the meaning of 'love' which many might be very comfortable with:

> 'Do I not hate those who hate you, O LORD?
> And do I not loathe those who rise up against you?
> I hate them with complete hatred;
> I count them my enemies.'

In His sermon on the values of the Kingdom of Heaven, Jesus seeks to counter a misguided understanding of what love is. It is not, He says, love towards your friends and hatred to your enemies; nor is it love towards those who love you or even the love shared within the family. For, as He says, even the tax collectors (Matthew 5:46) and Gentiles (vs. 47) do the same. Rather, it is to love the way the Father loves – indiscriminately (vs. 45).

The passage reads: 'You have heard that it was said, "You shall love your neighbour and hate your enemy." But I say to you, Love your enemies and pray for those who persecute you, so that you may be sons of your Father who is in heaven. For he makes his sun rise on the evil and on the good, and sends rain on the just and on the unjust. For if you love those who love you, what reward do you have? Do not even the tax collectors do the same? And if you greet only your brothers, what more are you doing than others? Do not even the Gentiles do the same? You therefore must be perfect, as your heavenly Father is perfect. (Matt. 5:43-48.)

These verses bring this section of the Sermon on the Mount to a climax. They call the believer to value the standards or characteristics of the Kingdom of Heaven.

Let's now explore some of the ingredients that need to be understood as we progress to Jesus' definition of love.

Firstly, this love requires **repentance**. According to Matthew 4:17, 'From that time Jesus began to preach, saying, *"Repent, for the kingdom of heaven is at hand."* '

When Jesus called His disciples, He did not simply tell them that *being generally nice and kind* is what love is. Nor did He suggest that the odd general adjustment of their lives and values so as to be in sync with the values of the Kingdom was what they needed. His message was, 'Repent' – turn around full circle because you are going the wrong way! Jesus is speaking to God-fearers! And to them He says, 'God's way is in contrast to all you know or think or have been taught! Repent!'

In the sermon He underlines a radical reversal of their understanding of love by saying that 'love' is not the way they have been taught – 'Ye have heard it that it was said . . . but. . . .' See Matthew 5:21-22, 27-28, 31-32, 33-34, 38-39, 43-44, KJV.

Secondly, this love requires **courage**. Matthew 5:3-12 has the Beatitudes as follows:

'Blessed are the poor in spirit, for theirs is the kingdom of heaven.

'Blessed are those who mourn, for they shall be comforted.

'Blessed are the meek, for they shall inherit the earth.

'Blessed are those who hunger and thirst for righteousness, for they shall be satisfied.

'Blessed are the merciful, for they shall receive mercy.

'Blessed are the pure in heart, for they shall see God.

'Blessed are the peacemakers, for they shall be called sons of God.

'Blessed are those who are persecuted for righteousness'

sake, for theirs is the kingdom of heaven.
'Blessed are you when others revile you and persecute you
and utter all kinds of evil against you falsely on my
account. Rejoice and be glad, for your reward is great in
heaven, for so they persecuted the prophets who were
before you.'

The benefits of being a citizen of that kingdom are included – we will be comforted, receive the earth, be satisfied, receive mercy, see God and be called sons of God. These are all part and parcel of receiving the Kingdom of Heaven. But we must be careful not to forget that the rewards are also virtues, and that they come at the cost of persecution! In other words, if you want to *'be sons of your Father who is in heaven'* (vs. 45), courage will be necessary.

Does it not take courage at times to walk across the street or room to express love to someone despised by the rest of the group? This love, it seems, may require the courage to act contrary to the prevailing expectations or norms of the culture we find ourselves in (*'You have heard that it was said . . .'*). As you try to embed the Father's kind of love into your lifestyle, prayers for courage, rather than deliverance from difficult situations, may be the order of your day.

Thirdly, this love requires **fulfilment**. When meeting the argument, which Jesus ran into many times (Mark 3:1-6 and John 9:16), that caring for people with love and compassion acts contrary to the Law, He countered by pointing out that rather than negating the Law, the values of the Kingdom, rightly lived, fill the Law full of meaning.

'Do not think that I have come to abolish the Law or the
Prophets; I have not come to abolish them but to fulfil

them. For truly, I say to you, until heaven and earth pass
away, not an iota, not a dot, will pass from the Law until
all is accomplished. Therefore whoever relaxes one of the
least of these commandments and teaches others to do the
same will be called least in the kingdom of heaven, but
whoever does them and teaches them will be called great
in the kingdom of heaven. For I tell you, unless your
righteousness exceeds that of the scribes and Pharisees,
you will never enter the kingdom of heaven.' Matt.
5:17-20.

The Father's love is not merely a matter of outward
appearances – like that of the scribes and Pharisees – who
exhibited their religion by saying and doing all the right
things but with a critical attitude towards others that was not
helpful. Instead of this the Father's love fulfils the Law at a
deeper level – inside our hearts (Matt. 5:20) – at the only
place we really become a part of the Kingdom of Heaven.

J. B. Phillips paraphrased this love beautifully: *'This love*
of which I speak is slow to lose patience – it looks for
a way of being constructive. It is not possessive: it is neither
anxious to impress nor does it cherish inflated ideas of its own
importance. Love has good manners and does not
pursue selfish advantage. It is not touchy. It does not keep
account of evil or gloat over the wickedness of other people. On
the contrary, it is glad with all good men when truth
prevails. Love knows no limit to its endurance, no end to its
trust, no fading of its hope; it can outlast anything. It is, in fact,
the one thing that still stands when all else has fallen.' (1 Cor.
13:4-8.)

The challenge is to ask yourself the question: 'How full is
my life of this kind of love?'

Fourthly, this love requires a form of **assertiveness**. In the sermon in Matthew 5 there follow several examples of the way the Father's kind of love operates.

> '*So if you are offering your gift at the altar and there remember that your brother has something against you, leave your gift there before the altar and go. First be reconciled to your brother, and then come and offer your gift. . . . If your right eye causes you to sin, tear it out and throw it away. . . . And if your right hand causes you to sin, cut it off and throw it away. . . . But I say to you that every-one who divorces his wife, except on the ground of sexual immorality, makes her commit adultery, and whoever marries a divorced woman commits adultery. . . . Let what you say be simply "Yes" or "No"; anything more than this comes from evil. . . . But if anyone slaps you on the right cheek, turn to him the other also . . . let him have your cloak as well . . . go with him two miles. Give to the one who begs from you, and do not refuse the one who would borrow from you. [Our Father] makes his sun rise on the evil and on the good, and sends rain on the just and on the unjust.*' Matthew 5:23-45.

When you read these verses through you encounter tough, brave, rugged, 'turn-your-cheek', assertive love. It is not just love when it suits us or to those we like or love, or who reciprocate. It is not soft, submissive, doormat love . . . it is principled love. It is the kind that says resolutely: 'You seek to crush me with your oppression and humiliation, but I will fight you with love!' This love is proactive – assertive.

Someone might argue that if we treat those who wish to harm us well – even while they are intent on doing evil (vs. 39) – we are in danger of showing complicity while permitting them to do their evil.

No! This love combats the evil, for it is precisely by loving them that we overcome those 'depraved' and 'detestable' sinners.

What if two men or two women or a pair of cross-dressers or transgender people walked in to church holding hands and then sat in church with their arms around each other – would that modify your 'love'?

Would you want to straighten them out before showing them the depth of the Father's love?

No! We combat the wrong not by straightening them out, but by loving them!

Doesn't God's love come to us that way – even 'while we were still sinners' (Rom. 5:8) and 'while we were enemies' (Rom. 5:10)?

I know of a non-Adventist church that does not have a health message but whose members make all their potluck meals vegetarian – so that even the vegetarian feels welcome. They are not teetotallers either, and yet they have banned all alcohol from their building because they want recovering alcoholics to feel supported there. That's assertive love.

Fifthly, this love is **excessive**. Listen to how Jesus expands on the theme of letting your love 'exceed that of the scribes and Pharisees': *'You have heard that it was said, "You shall love your neighbour and hate your enemy." But I say to you, Love your enemies and pray for those who persecute you, so that you may be sons of your Father who is in heaven. For he makes his sun rise on the evil and on the good, and sends rain on the just and on the unjust. For if you love those who love you, what reward do you have? Do not even the tax collectors do the same?*

*And if you greet only your brothers, what more are you
doing than others? Do not even the Gentiles do the same? You
therefore must be perfect, as your heavenly Father is perfect.'*
(Matt. 5:43-48.)

Here Jesus challenges us to love better than *'those who
love you'*, better than the *'tax collectors do'*, better than *'your
brothers'* do and better than *'the Gentiles do'*. The model held
up to us is the perfect love of *'your heavenly Father'*.

How does He love? Indiscriminately: *'For he makes his sun
rise on the evil and on the good, and sends rain on the just and
on the unjust.'* Yes, indiscriminately and excessively – like the
woman who throws a party for a lost coin wherein the party
cost more than the coin was worth! Like the father who runs
out to meet his prodigal son and then kills not just an
ordinary calf, but the fatted calf for him; or the shepherd
who throws a party for a lost sheep he has found – ever
heard of a shepherd doing that?

Here is the challenge to be creative – to think outside
the box – to practise abundant, wasteful, indiscriminate,
excessive love!

I learned of a lady in one of our churches who befriended
a young woman who had begun attending services but could
only afford to come in jeans and work clothes – it was all she
had. The lady befriended the young woman and arranged to
meet her in the local mall one day, where she took her to a
store and invited her to choose any clothes she wanted so
she could dress beautifully for church. When this was done
they went to the cashier where the lady kindly paid for it all!
That's the Father's kind of excessive love.

Chapter 4

Stories of misplaced value leadership

James Coffin tells this story: 'A few years ago I was standing in the foyer of a church when a young woman walked in wearing tight blue jeans, heavy makeup, a lot of jewellery, and a leather jacket. As she stood timidly, unsure what to do next, an elderly greeter walked over to her and asked, "Are you a man or a woman?" The girl looked at the greeter and stammered, "I'm . . . I'm a woman."

' "Then why don't you dress like one?" the greeter asked. The girl turned and headed for the door. I never saw her again.'

A pastor and his wife have a beloved son who grows into adulthood, leaves home and, sadly, drifts away from church. The couple pray earnestly for him and do all they can to tell him he is loved. One day the pastor has a preaching appointment in the town where he knows the son is living. He sends an email telling him of the appointment and how he would love to see him if he is able. There is no reply but the pastor goes in hope. During Sabbath School he keeps looking to see if the son turns up. He doesn't. Divine Service time comes. The preacher is now sitting on the platform with the other leaders and from his seat he is able to see through some side windows to the car park. His heart pounds with joy when he sees a car pull up, park and out steps his son – with a young lady at his side. He sees them walk towards the church entrance, then loses sight of them. He watches the entry door to the sanctuary but then is dismayed when, through the window, he sees them walk back to the car and drive away.

He completes his sermon and at the end of the service hurries to the foyer. There he meets a deacon and asks if he noticed a young man and woman come and then leave church. The deacon replies, 'Oh yes, and did you see the length of her miniskirt! I told her to go home and get dressed properly before she comes to this church.'

A pastor and his wife are enjoying a holiday. On Friday they scour the neighbourhood of their hotel to see if they can find a church to worship in on Sabbath, but they are not successful. So on Sabbath they dress casually, pack a small meal, their lesson book and Bible and decide to find a peaceful spot to enjoy Sabbath on their own. On the way they notice well-dressed people with Bibles under their arms and conclude that if they follow them they will find an Adventist church. Sure enough they find the church. Delighted, they walk up the steps to the entrance when a deacon steps forward and asks them where they are going. The pastor replies that they would like to worship in the church. The deacon says, 'You cannot come to worship dressed like that.' While the pastor seeks to explain that they are on holiday and had unexpectedly found the church, another gentleman steps forward and recognises the pastor, having seen him in a training programme. The friend introduces the pastor and his wife to the deacon, whereupon the deacon says, 'You are still not coming into church dressed like that!'

A couple visit a church. They are early and find seats fairly close to the front of the church. Moments before Sabbath School begins another couple come to them and tell them that they must move because these are their seats. The couple apologise and obligingly move a few rows back to some other seats. A few minutes later they are told by another couple that they must move because these are where they sit. Finally the visiting couple find themselves in a row near the back, not far from the tempting exit.

Here is the question that needs considering. Why did the greeter, the deacon, and those members do that? If you asked them if they intended to chase people away from Christ they would be shocked that you even thought that. 'Of course not!' they would exclaim.

Then why? What were the values that led them to say and do what they did? Let me hazard a suggestion. They valued dress standards and were trying to honour and respect the interior of the church. They also valued their particular seating arrangements during worship. You could argue that they valued their church and their worship highly. Good values? Of course they are. Don't we value and want people to demonstrate respect for holy things?

We could go on to ask similar questions about the need for people to stop eating meat, listening to bad music and lyrics, or drinking alcohol, etc. These are all good values, and they have their appropriate place. Our problem is, however, that they often get emphasised at the wrong time and place. Somehow we let them displace the really important values. By doing this we create invisible hoops through which visitors must jump before they are made welcome or can have access to the Gospel of grace that we want our church service to share with them. Grace then becomes something only for those we deem to have met our valued standards. I think God might not agree with this.

Yet we do sense that some values need to be held in abeyance until an appropriate time in a person's growth. I have no accounts (yet) of any deacon greeting a visitor with the words, 'Welcome to our church – do you eat pork?' or, 'Welcome to our church – have you treated your spouse kindly this week?' These are both good values, but we recognise that to confront visitors with such greetings is both inappropriate and evidence of a misplaced order of values. It places obstacles before the visitor, preventing them from receiving the Gospel and denying them access to the primary or exceeding values of the Kingdom. In later chapters we will consider how to properly prioritise our values so as to allow those who seek Jesus to find Him.

Chapter 5

It has got to stop

The stories in the previous chapter should make our blood boil. This has got to stop! These incidents are chasing away from Christ the very people we are seeking to win to Him. There is nothing of a sweet savour of life unto life in these stories. We are closing the door of the Kingdom to others and not partaking of the Kingdom ourselves. (Matt. 23:13.)

It is bad enough that we do it to strangers, but we even do it to our own people. A friend recounted to me the circumstances that led to him arriving late at church one day: his wife had suddenly come down with a terrible migraine; one of the children was ill and the hope of a pleasant Sabbath rest was shattered. That is why he was late for church, but at the door he was greeted with a gruff 'You are late!' My friend told me that had it not been for the 'duties' he had at church that day he would have turned around and gone home.

It has got to stop!

I have a copy of a quite lengthy letter that a young person let me read. I share it here as representative of how many of our people feel – people who just can't take it any more and leave.

'I stopped going to church about five years ago. I don't remember exactly. I was living in this little town where my dad had a house he was trying to sell. He'd been the teacher at the Adventist school and the people there had been incredibly nasty to him and the other teacher. They couldn't fire either teacher (they had no reason to), so they were so nasty that both he and the other teacher relocated. I knew what nasty people they could be, but I kept going to church anyway . . . even though only a handful of people would talk to me. The weirdest part of this story, though, is that they loved to stand up in church during the 'sharing' period and go on and on and on about what a friendly church it was and how glad they were that they were so enlightened (they didn't use that word though, too 'new agey') and didn't have such a dour, unfriendly church. Man, I hate hypocrisy. So I started looking for other Seventh-day Adventist churches; I found one that was racially diverse, wasn't all rich white people, and where the people were really, genuinely friendly . . . but the pastor. One of his sermons was a laundry list of things that bugged him (people wearing hats in the sanctuary, people being late to church – said just as a woman with five kids stumbled in . . . late). . . . In another sermon he mentioned that he wished all gay people would just go back in the closet (the last time I attended that church) . . . it was an incredibly hateful thing to say. For a long time I'd started looking outside of Adventism, but my experiences with these two churches pretty much killed any desire to be a part of organised religion. And I haven't been. At times I miss the community of being in a church . . . but it's just not worth it to me. The culture and the tradition kept me going, it was something that felt familiar and comfortable . . . until it wasn't comfortable anymore.'

It has got to stop!

They are our children that we are pushing away. We are pushing them out and closing the door to them and by our words and actions demonstrating that we are not part of the Kingdom anyway.

Is there any hope?

The same letter – quite a way towards its end – gives us a glimpse of an organisation that is values-led. Read what she wrote . . .

'Let me just say, though, that I think ADRA is the one thing Adventists are doing right – it's not an organisation out to "convert" the masses . . . it's there to HELP people, individuals, and I truly believe that they do it better than most. There's an emphasis on sustainable economies, protecting the environment, helping women and children, etc . . . but as far as sitting in the pews each week is concerned, compassion is not a reality. At least not the pews I was sitting in.'

What if we as individuals were disciplined in being values-led? What if compassionate service were the passionate value that motivated our actions? I don't for a moment think we can do this all the time and in every action – we are after all sinners and our default mode is self-centredness – but what if we aspired to that? What if we were so passionate about it that we were willing to be made accountable in our communities of faith to each other and we sought to inspire each other to compassionate service to others? As Paul put it in Romans 12:10-17: *'Love one another with brotherly affection. Outdo one another in showing honour. Do not be slothful in zeal, be fervent in spirit, serve the Lord. Rejoice in hope, be patient in tribulation, be constant in prayer. Contribute to the needs of the saints and seek to show hospitality. Bless those who persecute you; bless and do not curse them. Rejoice with those who rejoice, weep with those who weep. Live in harmony with one another. Do not be haughty, but associate with the lowly. Never be wise in your own sight. Repay no one evil for evil, but give thought to do what is honourable in the sight of all.'*

I wonder how many other young people (and others) in our churches might wish they had the courage to write a similar letter to tell us their true feelings – or is it just easier to walk quietly away?

Our churches must stop the kinds of behaviour that are driving people away and start living the values of the Kingdom we belong to. Does anyone know how to do it? I would like to be a part of that community!

Chapter 6

Our secret that the world knows and we have forgotten

Research by health scientists has, in recent years, caught up with something we have known for decades – that the eight principles of healthy living are the best formula for health and longevity. We are delighted that the world is cottoning on to one of our secrets. What took them so long!

But there is another church secret that we seem to have forgotten and that the world is ahead of us on. After all, didn't Jesus warn us that 'the children of this world are in their generation wiser than the children of light' (Lk 16:8, KJV)? Lovett Weems, in his book *Church Leadership*, writes that a 'great surprise for church leaders when they begin reading supposedly secular books about leadership is that the language used in the best of the books seems to come directly from the vocabulary of the church. They expect to find elaborate grids, schemes, and designs. Instead, they discover words that have to do with values and character. It soon becomes quite evident that there is no way to talk about leadership without talking about values, meaning, and personhood. The character and values of the leader do matter.'

Secular studies have come to the conclusion that an

organisation without values (particularly one that claims to be of service to others) has no future.

Robert Greenleaf in his *Servant Leadership* (Paulist Press, 1977) tells the tale of Leo, who is employed by a group of mythical explorers. Leo is the servant who takes care of all the menial tasks but who always does so with a cheerful spirit and encouraging songs. All goes well until Leo disappears. The party falls into disarray and eventually the expedition is abandoned. One of the group wanders about for some time and then discovers an order where the noble and great leader is none other than Leo.

The point of the story is that organisations that do not embed servant leadership are doomed to failure.

Peter Block in his book *Stewardship*, written for the secular business world, says: 'Most businesses got the point in the 1970s and 1980s: if they did not find a way to serve their markets more quickly, with higher quality and lower costs, they would not endure.' Note the key word, 'serve'. No service – no future.

And they have recognised that those values must be intentionally internalised or embedded into all they do. Their stated values are what they do. It's not just a nice idea that is vaguely and occasionally done.

One company that posted superb values was Enron. It openly stated that *Communication, Respect, Integrity* and *Excellence* were what it stood for. Events subsequent to Enron's collapse revealed that these actually covered an embedded cultural value of greed. Various books and numerous articles (easily accessed online) document this tragic betrayal of values.

A company that the 'children of light' would do well to consider is Southwest Airlines – an inspirational American business that demonstrates the effect of its values by being the company with the lowest number of complaints, the highest customer loyalty, plus never having recorded a loss in its history.

Ken Makovsky in a *Forbes.com* article[1] describes Southwest's three core values as follows: 'The values transcend the more typical ones, such as "Take the initiative" or "Care about your customers." ' **A warrior spirit**, according to Ms Hardage [Southwest Airlines' cultural executive and chief communications officer], means being fearless in terms of delivering the product. "We need to give our employees all the tools they need to support our customers. People travel for a variety of reasons – business, funerals, vacations – and you need to be sensitive to their space and schedules."

'**A servant's heart** also fits right in. Treat others with respect. Follow the Golden Rule. Put other people first. "We believe we need to connect people to what is important in their lives through friendly, reliable and low-cost air travel. If you respect their concerns and needs, and still provide low-cost and low-fare terms, then you do indeed have a servant's heart. The customer, hopefully, is getting more than he or she paid for."

'And, of course, **a "fun-luving" attitude.** "We want people who are proud to be here, people who have a fun and 'luving' attitude and don't take themselves too seriously. Our culture is defined by these three values, and they are used as the cardinal test for newly hired employees, who have to reflect those values." '

I would recommend to all church leaders to take a little time reading about Southwest – in literature and online. Their commitment to excellence, service and 'luv' (as they spell the word) is simply inspiring and I would humbly submit that we as members, leaders and churches would not go far wrong in learning some of the wisdom of these 'children of this world'.

One of the stories that I liked that demonstrated Southwest's commitment to its values was one about a customer who wrote in to the company complaining about the levity (in Southwest's terms – 'fun-luving attitude') evidenced on the flight they had taken. The letter was passed on to the CEO. A usual reply might have been apologetic, but not Herb Kelleher's reply – he simply wrote back, 'We'll miss you.'

Kelleher is quoted as saying: *'You can't really be disciplined in what you do unless you are humble and open-minded. Humility breeds open-mindedness – and, really, what we try to do is establish a clear and simple set of values that we understand. That simplifies things; that expedites things. It enables the extreme discipline I mentioned in describing our strategy. When an issue comes up, we don't say we're going to study it for two and a half years. We just say, "Southwest Airlines doesn't do that. Maybe somebody else does, but we don't." It greatly facilitates the operation of the company.*[2]

What amazes me as I read such literature about secular companies are the words that they use to describe themselves. Words like 'service', 'servant', 'disciplined', 'humble', 'songs', 'spirit', 'excellence', 'commitment', 'care'. They are using our terminology – the words that describe our basis for Kingdom success. It comes across to me that they have learned something that we have forgotten.

Now here are some questions that this wisdom of the

world raises for the children of light.

Reader, what are your core values?

What are the enunciated values of your church?

What were the values behind the sad stories in the fourth chapter of this little book?

Is there a disconnect between the values we espouse and the values that we act on?

Do some of our actions betray the values of the Kingdom we claim?

In our next chapter we will share a handful of stories from secular organisations, one of which is described as having 'exemplary corporate culture, exceptional staff empowerment, and extraordinary commitment' (watch out for the quote!). Could you use those same adjectives to describe yourself or the church you attend? If not, why not?

Be encouraged – if the world can excel there is no reason why we can't do even better. What an amazing church that would be – we would fly!

[1] *http://www.forbes.com/sites/kenmakovsky/2013/11/21/behind-the-southwest-airlines-culture/*
[2] *http://www.strategy-business.com/article/04212?pg=all*

Chapter 7

Stories of value

A Google search under 'customer satisfaction stories' and 'company value statements' could fill this chapter with links and give you hours of reading. Let me share a few that impressed me.

Some of my favourites come from Nordstrom customers. Nordstrom is a retailer of quality footwear, clothing, jewellery, home accessories and other goods, a company that claims to be the number-one in customer service. (See *The Nordstrom Way* by R. Spector and P. McCarthy, John Wiley & Sons, 1995.) By the way – empowering staff with responsibility is the reason there are no 'complaints departments' in the Nordstrom organisation – each employee is the customer complaints department!

A woman in a North Carolina Nordstrom store lost a diamond from her wedding ring while trying on clothes in the store. Naturally, she began to search for it on her knees, scouring the floor. A store worker saw her, and after finding what she was doing joined her on his knees searching for the diamond. After some time the worker asked two other workers to join them in their search. One of them suggests that the floor will have been cleaned, so they open up the vacuum bags of two machines that were used and find the missing shining jewel. That is another happy customer whose loyalty to the shop has been strongly encouraged.

Here is another story of a man in Portland who wanted an Armani tuxedo for his daughter's wedding. Unable to locate one, he finally tries Nordstrom. The attendant takes his measurements and the next day phones to say that they have found the tuxedo and that it will be ready the following day. The attendant had had the tux altered for free and the man found it fitted exactly. The impressed man quizzed the attendant to find out how she had accomplished it. She explained that through connections she had located the tux on the other side of the country in New York and arranged, via a number of connections, to have it delivered and altered for the customer. So what is really so amazing about that service? Nordstrom doesn't sell Armani tuxedos!

But it's not only Nordstrom that impress with their customer service: here are a couple of stories that show service involving children.

Go to ASDA or Tesco and you will find tiger bread, but not in Sainsbury's, where it is called giraffe bread. Why? Here is the story. In 2013, three-and-a-half-year-old Lily Robinson was shopping with her mother in Sainsbury's when she noticed that what her mum called tiger bread (named after the pattern on the bread crust) looked much more like the skin markings of a giraffe. Lily's mother agreed and encouraged her to write to Sainsbury's, asking why it was called tiger bread instead of giraffe bread.

Chris King, who was on the store customer service team, responded to Lily's letter as follows: 'Renaming tiger bread giraffe bread is a brilliant idea – it looks much more like the blotches on a giraffe than the stripes on a tiger, doesn't it?' Lily's mother posted the letters on her blog and some time later they became the topic of thousands of comments on Twitter and Facebook. Sainsbury's changed the name of the bread and received hundreds of posts and calls commending them on a great piece of customer service.

As noted in the previous chapter, Southwest Airlines is a US-based airline that leads in customer satisfaction. Commentators on Southwest claim that they lead with the fewest complaints of any airline and the highest customer loyalty. Why? Southwest considers itself a customer service business that happens to be in the flying business. Integral to that is a conviction that love of fun or 'luv' of fun, as they call it, combined with the freedom for staff to take responsibility in the way they treat customers, gives their employees the ability to make a flight an enjoyable experience.

For example, when a group of students travelling together on a Southwest flight asked to help, the hostess saw an opportunity to make their flight an enjoyable and memorable one. The stewardess allowed them to serve the peanuts to the people on the plane. One of the students explained who they were and his classmates joined in serving the passengers, who enjoyed the students' attention. The crew were pleased to have them help. The pilot awarded them all with 'wings' and they had their pictures taken with the staff, and it goes without saying that the students will never forget their experience.

Stories abound – many outstanding and many simple. Here is one from Joseph A. Michelli's book, *The New Gold Standard* (McGraw-Hill, 2008), in which he '. . . reveals the specific leadership behaviours that produce Ritz-Carlton Hotel's exemplary corporate culture, exceptional staff empowerment, and extraordinary commitment to its customers' (page 2). It is a simple story, but one that illustrates the service attitude of this organisation. 'A guest was getting ready for an early-morning meeting that was to happen in a matter of hours when the guest realised he had forgotten his formal dress shoes. The man asked Mark [the hotel concierge agent on duty] if there was any place that he could get a pair of shoes at that hour. Mark advised that no stores were open prior to the start of the guest's meeting. As Mark searched for a solution, he found out that the man's shoe size matched his own. Mark offered to bring the guest a pair of formal shoes that he had worn only at his wedding. When the guest accepted the offer, Mark raced home and brought the shoes back to the hotel.' (Page 197.)

Let me finish this section with another Nordstrom tale.

A businessman travelling between cities damaged his suit jacket and needed it repaired at short notice. Unable to find a repairer who could have it ready the next day, he recalled his wife's advice to 'go to Nordstrom'. The man had never shopped at Nordstrom before and got to the store shortly before it closed, only to be told that there is usually a 24-hour turnaround for such repairs. Nevertheless, the service attendant says he will try to have it the next day. At 9am the next morning the man arrives at the store on his way to the airport to find that the jacket is not there. The attendant makes arrangements to mail it to his home. The man catches the plane to his next destination, goes about his business appointments, then finds the hotel he is booked into. On entering his room he finds the suit plus a shirt and tie and a note from Nordstrom saying they had contacted his wife, found the hotel address and forwarded the suit to him – the shirt and tie were complimentary. The man ends his testimony by saying that he is now a Nordstrom customer.

Chapter 8

What a man's got to do

There is some uncertainty about the origin of the line, 'A man's got to do what a man's got to do'. Some believe John Steinbeck penned it, but others say it is near enough to something that John Wayne rasps out in one of his gritty movies. Whoever said it first is uncertain, but there is no question about who lived it fully.

Jesus' first recorded words reveal a remarkable focus on what He came to do. His parents lost Him and after three days they discovered Him in the temple. To His mother's distressed question, with its implied rebuke – 'Son, why have you treated us so?' (Luke 2:48) – the Boy Jesus responds with surprise, astonished that His parents did not know where He would be: 'And he said unto them, How is it that ye sought me? wist ye not that I must be about my Father's business?' (Luke 2:49, KJV.)

Little is clearer in Jesus' focus of what He has to do than this commitment to doing His Father's will.

Early in His ministry Jesus is confronted with a public relations opportunity. It is a Sunday morning and 'everyone' from the town is early and eagerly seeking Him, but He has risen even earlier to find a place of prayer. The record says that 'Simon and those who were with him searched for him, and they found him and said to him, "Everyone is looking for you." ' (Mark 1:36-37.) 'Apparently,' comments Vincent Taylor, 'they thought that Jesus was losing a great opportunity afforded by the healings and exorcisms at Capernaum.' To their surprise Jesus dismisses the opportunity, choosing rather to do what He came to do. 'And he saith unto them, Let us go elsewhere into the next towns, that I may preach there also; for to this end came I forth' (Mark 1:38, RV). As someone once quipped, 'Jesus knew that the main thing is keeping the main thing the main thing.'

On one occasion, after feeding the multitude, the crowd and the disciples seek to make Jesus their king. It is a route to the Kingdom that is as unacceptable to Jesus as when the devil offered the world to Jesus during the wilderness temptations. He firmly orders the disciples to leave and then 'commands the multitude to disperse; and His manner is so decisive that they dare not disobey. The words of praise and exaltation die on their lips. In the very act of advancing to seize Him their steps are stayed, and the glad, eager look fades from their countenances.' (Ellen White, *The Desire of Ages*, page 378.) Jesus brooks no consideration of an alternative route from that which He has got to do.

Each of the synoptic gospels refers to the determination of Jesus to go to Jerusalem to die. The phrase 'stedfastly set his face' in Luke's account (Luke 9:51, KJV) aptly captures His intentions. Mark (Mark 10:32) augments that with his picture of Jesus striding out towards Jerusalem while the disciples dally along behind, amazed and fearful. Peter's rebuke to Jesus' intentions in Matthew 16:21-23 elicits a powerful rejection by the Saviour of the satanic idea that He should avoid the things that God expects from Him.

Nowhere in the Word is there a stronger demonstration of

Jesus' commitment to the Father's will than is found in the account of what happened between Gethsemane and His death on the cross: while the Father turns His face away, His human companions sleep while He needs their supporting prayers; while satanic agencies press in close to torment Him. His humanity is tested and He cries for escape from the dark horror that surrounds Him. It even seems that His Father has turned His face away . . . but bravely He reaffirms His choice: 'Thy will be done!'

Why? Why this passionate determination? The apostle John answers it simply – love. It is the core value of the character of God (1 John 4:8). It is the value that most often evidences itself in His relationship to the world (John 3:16). It is the value upon which hangs His law (Matt. 22:40). It is the value that, when acted on and out, fulfils the law (Rom. 13:10). It is the guiding and defining value of the Kingdom of God.

Jesus chose to do what He did because He was driven by that core value of the Father. All of His life is a revelation of the Father's value-led character. But He does what He does not simply because He is obeying an external rule of some sort, but because He shares the nature of the Godhead. It is an embedded and intentionally acted-on part of who He is. He does what His nature is – He is true to Himself. He is the Man who does what a man's got to do. Yet it is not only to Himself that He is true – in His humanity He submits Himself obediently to the Father, for in His life and death He 'proves God's great love for man' (Ellen White, *The Acts of the Apostles*, page 209).

When Jesus submitted Himself to this life choice, two questions arose: 'why' and 'how'? These are questions we ask with every challenge we face. 'Analytics helps answer the 'how question' – how to use resources efficiently, detect opportunities, compare costs, and so on. But to answer the 'why question' – why this matters, why we care, why we value one goal over another – we turn to narrative. The why question is not why we think we ought to act, but rather, why we do act, that which actually moves us to act, our motivation, our values. Or, as St Augustine wrote, it is 'the difference between "knowing" the good, an ought, and "loving the good", a source of motivation'.[1]

In the Garden of Gethsemane, when His humanity cries for release from the cup, He recognises the implications this has for the rest of humanity and submits Himself to drink its woe and trust His life into the hands of the cup Holder. His other-centred, love-led heart chose to be true to His own values and those of Heaven and give Himself for the redemption of mankind. We are bought at a cost – the precious blood of Christ (1 Cor. 6:20; 1 Pet. 1:19). Why? He did what His nature's response was. He did what the Man's got to do.

Christ's example sets the values standard of those who claim to belong to that same Kingdom.

From the pen of Ellen White we read, 'It is the fragrance of our love for our fellow men that reveals our love for God' (*The Acts of the Apostles*, page 560).

'The children of the Heavenly King should represent the character of the Ruler of the heavenly kingdom. They should cultivate unity and love for one another, each member of the royal family loyally representing the principles of the government of God. Jesus Christ was sent of God. In His character and life He represented every principle of the law of God. What are the two great principles of that law? Love to God and love to our neighbours. We are to cherish a warm, deep, abiding interest in one another, an unfeigned respect for our brethren and sisters. We are none of us to set ourselves up as critics, to discern defects in those with whom we associate, and then engage in a work of cannibalism, tearing to pieces the reputation of those who may be more precious in the sight of God than we are. Evil thinking and evil speaking are a great offence in the sight of God, and those who do those things are not born of the Spirit but of the flesh. (Manuscript 19, 17 March 1894, par. 14.)

Again, 'There can be no more conclusive evidence that we possess the spirit of Satan than the disposition to hurt and destroy those who do not appreciate our work, or who act contrary to our ideas.' (*The Desire of Ages*, page 487.)

It is time for the men (and women) of the Kingdom to do what 'a man (or woman) has got to do'.

[1]Marshall Ganz, 'Leading Change: Leadership, Organisation, and Social Movements', chapter 19 in Nitin Nohria and Rekesh Khurana, Editors: *Handbook of Leadership Theory and Practice*, 26 January, 2010.

Where can they go to see the Kingdom of God?

S teve Logan, a scientist living in bonnie Scotland and a member of Crieff Seventh-day Adventist Church, once challenged me with a question that is the title of this chapter: Where can people go to see the Kingdom of God? Steve continued to press his point by saying that we cannot send them down to the local supermarket to ask for a packet of it.

How would you answer the question?

This should be a straightforward rhetorical question, with an obvious answer – the local church, of course! But the answer does not easily trip off the tongue. Many that I have asked the question to shrug their shoulders and, with palms upturned, nod and whisper what they think is the right answer, thus acknowledging that there is a problem.

As I have thought about the matter, I see three issues.

Firstly – and I understand this to be Steve's point – that, unlike supermarkets, we at church can and do place obstacles in the path of the Kingdom-seeker. Steve writes as follows, 'If Fred hits hard times and starts looking around for a reason to exist, then, hopefully, he'll think about maybe possibly popping in to that building he passes on the way to work – the one with the steeple and the big sign outside saying "Welcome". So he plucks up his courage and wanders in on a Sabbath morning. What happens now? Does the man on the door look him up and down and tut-tut at the inappropriate attire? Does he "accidentally" sit in one of the chairs that "everyone" knows belong to the Smith family? Does Fred get identified by a man on the platform and hailed, in an ever-so-friendly way, as a "guest"? None of these things would happen were Fred to go looking for any other product or service. Which is my point: if you're a "seeker", and we (the church) are hoping to attract "seekers", then we have to be aware of those things we do that are, frankly, a bit nuts to an outsider. We, the church, are the purveyors of "the Meaning of Life", and there is literally *nothing* we should insert between he who seeks and He who provides.'

Please compare what Steve writes to my fourth chapter above on misplaced values.

The second issue is the anomaly that at times it is easier to see the values of the Kingdom of Heaven in the 'supermarket' than in the church. Two examples of the secular practice of Kingdom values come to mind.

A recent book by Joseph Michelli entitled *The New Gold Standard* outlines the Ritz-Carlton embedded culture of non-judgemental and generous service (see chapter 20 of this book). The hotel chain makes the claim that it is the world's 'gold standard' in serving people. Shouldn't that be the Church's claim? Ritz-Carlton employees are proud of their organisation and its record of outstanding service that keeps its customers coming back for more. An example (and I choose this story because it is often in the small actions that a value is revealed) that Michelli relates is of a waitress who is asked by a girl in a family she is serving if they have a particular type of ice cream that doesn't appear on the menu. The waitress, instead of just giving a smiling apology (which surely would be fully acceptable), says, 'Let me see what I can do.' She then asks another waiter to cover her tables while she pops round to an ice cream shop she knows, buys the right type, rushes back to the hotel kitchen, and emerges with the other desserts plus the ice cream the girl asks for. That is gold-standard service. In answer to Steve's question about where to see the Kingdom of Heaven, dare the answer be, 'At a Ritz-Carlton hotel!'

The other example is the practices of people care that Nordstrom employees give to their customers. In reviewing the book, *The Nordstrom Way*, by Robert Spector and Patrick McCarthy, Tom Peters (a leadership guru) states that 'Nobody does it better than Nordstrom.' A Church reply should be, 'That's nonsense – we practise people care better than anyone!' After all, this is where the Kingdom values are to be seen.

One of Nordstrom's tools of trade is the personal customer book (see page 184 of the above book) that sales associates carry. In that small book the associate records all the details they can obtain about each person they serve – their names, phone number, purchases, likes and dislikes, etc. Eventually they build up a confidential dossier about each customer that enables them not only to remember their names the next time they visit the shop, but to relate with such personalised care that the customer seeks them out, knowing that they are cared for. What a lesson for our diaconate to learn. Sometimes we can't even remember our members' names, let alone those of any visitors and their children. I decided to trial Nordstrom's tool. At two churches that I visited, I recorded on my mobile phone the names and any identifying details of those I spoke to. At one church I recorded the names of 40 people I interacted with and at the other I wrote down about 15. As I had opportunity I reviewed the names and faces and was amazed that at the end of the service I was able to speak to most of them again using their first names. While writing this chapter I went to my phone record and found that I could still remember, almost a month later, 37 of the 40 names I had recorded in the first case and 14 of the 15 in the other. This was stunning, because I am terrible at remembering names. I even momentarily forgot my wife's name once! But the simple Nordstrom tool took me to a new level of Kingdom care – see Chapter 22 of this book, where I list some suggestions that may be helpful for deacons and others who are tasked with meeting and greeting at church. And again, the reply to Steve's question might be that we would do well to point seekers of the Kingdom of Heaven to the 'supermarket' rather than to some of our churches.

There may be some readers that may object to any comparison between the Church and secular organisations on the ground that they are the children of the world and not the children of light, and so cannot possibly represent the Kingdom of Heaven. My reply would be that Jesus Himself stated that 'the children of this world are in their generation wiser than the children of light' (Luke 16:8, KJV). He also found no greater faith in all Israel than He found in an army soldier, a pagan Roman centurion. When Jesus heard this, he marvelled and said to those who followed Him, 'Truly, I tell you, with no one in Israel have I found such faith' (Matt. 8:10).

It may be that I have created a wrong impression in implying that the Kingdom can only be seen in the Church. The reality may be that, just as Jesus saw examples of the

Kingdom everywhere they happened to appear, so we today may also find the Kingdom of Heaven wherever it erupts or invades our dark planet. Wherever we see the values of grace, mercy, humility, peace, purity, service, meekness, right actions, etc, manifested we should rejoice to see examples of the Kingdom of Heaven.

The third issue is the failure, at times, of the local church to be the place where the Kingdom can be seen. Surely it is here where the Kingdom of Heaven should be most easily seen. The church does not always fail. There are magnificent stories and examples of churches and members being marvellous windows into the Kingdom, but there are serious failures too. I am not expecting perfect churches, and we should keep in mind that there must certainly be customers who have had bad experiences with organisations like Ritz-Carlton and Nordstrom, but the difference that concerns me is that, while these 'supermarkets' can purposely embed values like exceptional service and customer care into the fabric of their culture, many of our churches struggle to do the same, let alone better. Here are some questions we need to ask ourselves. Why can Ritz-Carlton boast at being the best in giving service while we are often too proud to trumpet our commitment to being servants? Maybe it is not pride on our part; maybe it is embarrassment at failing to serve. And why can Nordstrom train its assistants to amazing levels of customer care while we struggle to make attendees feel amazingly welcome to our churches?

On exploring this issue with some churches the reply has come back that the secular organisations do it well because they are paid and motivated by a profit incentive. It would be a very sad commentary on our understanding of the

Gospel if we were to conclude that if we paid our deacons and deaconesses they would serve better. Maybe the world serves for profit, but who are we to judge? At least they give clear examples of doing it well. Assuming they serve well for an earthly crown, is not the 'unfading crown of glory' (1 Peter 5:4) that we aspire to worth much more? And is not the kingdom they aspire to a temporal and fading one, while ours is an eternal and glorious Kingdom?

It is not the local supermarket that aspires to represent the Kingdom of Heaven. That is the claim and privilege of the church. Even though supermarkets may provide glimpses into the values that belong to a better world, it is the church, worldwide and local, that has to be the window in the world to the values of the Kingdom. And so, too, shouldn't the local church be the place that intentionally aspires to be the place to see the Kingdom of Heaven at its best?

I am arguing that the church, worldwide and locally, has the divine responsibility of working out what the core and exceeding values of the Kingdom of Heaven are, stating and embedding them into its life and practice, then holding itself accountable to those values.

When the question is asked, 'Where can they see the Kingdom of Heaven on earth?' the answer should naturally come back, 'Let me invite you to my local church; we are not perfect, but we are a community totally committed to doing everything we can to evidence the values of the Kingdom of Heaven. Come and see for yourself!'

Chapter 10

But . . . when do we tell them to shape up?

Being values-led is not a matter of listing all the values one can think of that describe the Kingdom citizen and then scrapping all but the top few. It is more a matter of working out which are the ones that are the most important – the weightier ones – then letting them guide your life to start with.

Jesus pronounced woe to the scribes and Pharisees for their emphasis on pernickety tithing of tiny seeds and excessive cleanliness while discarding values such as justice, mercy and faith (Matt. 23:23-26). He went on to indicate that it was not that tithing and cleanliness were wrong, but that their upside-down value system demonstrated that their insides needed changing.

And there lies the problem with the enthusiastic greeter who tells the visitor to go home and dress properly before entering the church. The greeter cannot see that both he and the visitor need to be changed on the inside first, before they can be clean on the outside.

How else shall a person change? If they change because of fear or pressure they will only have changed on the outside. It is the love of God inside the heart that truly changes the inside. Do we not understand that it is the goodness, kindness, tolerance and patience of God that turns us around? (Rom. 2:4.)

A lady in the church asked me to help with some Bible studies for a young woman she had met. We eagerly went to her home and began the studies. There was a problem in that her boyfriend lived with her. We ignored that and began our studies, starting with the prophecy of Daniel 2 and leading on to the news about the coming of Jesus. Her boyfriend sat in on the studies. On about our third or fourth visit the lady asked if she could speak to us privately. It felt a little awkward going into her bedroom and leaving her boyfriend alone in the living room, but imagine our surprise when she told us that during her reviews of what we had studied the impression came to her mind that she could no longer live with her boyfriend in the same apartment. She asked if God expected that of her. We replied that she must ask God for wisdom in this matter. She was quiet for a short time and then said, 'I know what God wants me to do.' She then promptly went back into the living room and gently told the friend that he needed to find his own accommodation if they were to follow God. He did, and both later became members of the church. This lesson taught me that my work was to draw our contacts to the love of God and His truth, and allow the Holy Spirit to guide them in His own time.

On another occasion I called at a house in response to a card that had been sent in requesting Bible study guides. A young man opened the door, but upon learning why I had come apologised to me for the waste of my time, because he had filled the card in as a joke. He expected the lessons to come through the post and planned simply to bin them. Nevertheless, I explained the guides and the free Bible that came with them. He told me that he did not have a Bible and had never read it. I offered him a deal – if he would do the first two lessons he could keep the Bible and tell me not to return again the next week when I dropped in to see how he had got on. He laughed, and then added his own conditions to the deal. They were that under no conditions were the guides or I to tell him that alcohol and his sleeping around with many girls was wrong. Should I break those conditions I was not to bring any more guides. I agreed. I was shocked the next week when upon knocking on his door the young man practically dragged me into his house. 'These lessons are fantastic!' he exclaimed, 'I have never read anything like this.' A week or two later, armed with lessons 5 and 6, I called again. This time he had not just completed the lessons but was devouring the Scriptures. This continued for another couple of weeks until, after delivering the next pair of guides, he again shocked me by saying, 'Llew, God's Spirit has touched my heart and mind and I see that my misuse of girls for my sexual appetite is an abuse of them and alcohol is a large part of my lifestyle. I have decided to stop drinking completely and will not indulge in sex until I find the woman I want to marry.'

That day I vividly recall walking from his home amazed by what the Spirit of Christ can do. There and then I determined that with all I worked with I would uplift Christ and allow the rising sap of the Spirit of God to knock off the old leaves of a dead life.

'The precious blood of Jesus is the fountain prepared to cleanse the soul from the defilement of sin. When you determine to take Him as your friend, a new and enduring light will shine from the cross of Christ. A true sense of the sacrifice and intercession of the dear Saviour will break the heart that has become hardened in sin; and love, thankfulness, and humility will come into the soul. The surrender of the heart to Jesus subdues the rebel into a penitent, and then the language of the obedient soul is: "Old things are passed away; behold, all things are become new." This is the true religion of the Bible. Everything short of this is a deception.' (Ellen White, *Testimonies for the Church*, vol. 4, page 625.)

'But,' you ask, 'when do we tell them to shape up?' My answer is: 'You don't!'

My model is Christ. Go to the stories of Jesus' interaction with sinners and you will find that He does not tell them to 'shape up' (there is one exception, which I will come to). Rather, He eats and drinks with them (at Matthew's house); throws forgiveness at them (the man who comes down through the roof); calls active sinners to follow Him (Levi was sitting at his tax booth when Jesus called him from it); teaches that the father runs to embrace prodigals (Luke responds to each act of contrition by the son with a 'but the father . . .' – see Luke 15:20, 22). Jesus' condemnation of sins is clearly aimed at religious people, not sinners; the people who claim to be on the inside, not those on the outside.

Our work is not to condemn. We will not be judged on how well we told the sinners off. We will be excluded from the Kingdom by our failure to love them. Our great task is to live the core values of God's character. That is where we as individuals and churches must focus our efforts. Our critical focus must be on how well we are doing, not how badly they are doing. It is this outstanding love or steadfast mercy or amazing grace that we show that we must excel at.

Before we finish – that exception. In John 8:11 Jesus said to the woman, 'Go . . . and sin no more.' Let us be clear that this is prefaced by, 'Neither do I condemn you.' When I read this I wonder whether Jesus is ignorant of her sin, that He can brush it away so simply. Does He have nothing to condemn her for? Surely He knew her deeds . . . but as I read the story more and more I begin to wonder what sin He tells her not to fall into any more. The Pharisees said that it was adulterous behaviour. Might it be that He was warning her not to be led into sin by religious people who had groomed her for the situation she found herself in?

Chapter 11

The attitudes that exceed . . .

I once dropped several containers of vegetable seeds, got them all mixed up and ended up planting a row of mixed seeds in my allotment. Sure enough, I did not get all the same vegetables in that row. The DNA of each seed decided the vegetable that grew. Jesus tried to explain that in His lesson about a tree's fruit being determined by the kind of tree it is. On another occasion (Mark 7:23) He sought to explain to His slow-to-learn disciples that what comes out of a person is determined by what is in his heart. It is our own values, or seeds planted in our hearts, that determine our actions.

This illustration from nature doesn't fully hold true for humans, in that the seed or tree cannot change its own DNA. A lettuce seed cannot decide to bring forth a carrot or even a cabbage that may look somewhat similar. Humans can apparently choose their moral DNA. Jesus implied this when He stated that we can individually choose to exhibit righteous actions that differ from those used by others. The word He used is 'exceeds' – '. . . unless your righteousness exceeds that of the scribes and Pharisees, you will never enter the kingdom of heaven.' (Matthew 5:20.)

His statement is very challenging on two points.

Firstly – who would ever imagine being more righteous than a scribe or Pharisee? George Knight (*Turn Your Eyes Upon Jesus*, page 75) points out that the Pharisees were a 'select class of some 6,000 individuals who had totally dedicated their lives to bringing about the coming of the Christ through living sinless lives. . . . Pharisees were completely devoted to God's law. They loved it with all their heart. Their dedication to keeping it inspired them to formulate thousands of guidelines so that they wouldn't even come close to the appearance of evil. Thus they had some 1,521 oral rules on how to keep the Sabbath. Such laws touched every aspect of their lives.'

Secondly, the word 'never' allows for no exceptions. You don't sneak past this condition, as if one might argue that we can get through as an exception. The King James translation, 'in no case', closes the door on any other route into the Kingdom.

So what are the statement's implications, and how do you do better than a Pharisee?

I would like to propose that the Sermon on the Mount is an explanation of the values that characterise the Kingdom of Heaven. David Stern (*Jewish New Testament Commentary*, page 16) says that the word 'heaven' is a pious way of avoiding the word 'God'. So the theme of the sermon could be summarised as a description of who belongs to and who doesn't belong to the kingdom where God rules. Jesus takes the listener away from any legalistic definitions of Kingdom membership by pointing out that Kingdom people are 'sons of your Father who is in heaven' (Matt. 5:45, see also vs. 48). Hmmm . . . like Father, like Son . . . maybe nature's DNA analogy does have some things to teach us.

Jesus begins this famous sermon with a description of the

attitudes or values that characterise Kingdom people. We call that part the Beatitudes, and the word 'kingdom' is used more than once in them. Kingdom people are humble, they mourn over what sin has done, they are gentle, they ache for right to prevail, they love kindness, they have a passion for purity, they bring people together in community, and they don't waver from their values under pressure. These are not attitudes they wear just for the occasion. They are the relatives of a long line of Kingdom people. Jesus then describes their influence – they are like salt and light to their communities. They bring flavour to insipid living and hope to dark lives.

Imagine with me that there are Pharisees in the audience. Can you hear them murmuring to each other about the fact that Jesus has not included the Sabbath or cleanliness or tithing – He has ignored the Law, they argue!

Jesus reads their minds and says, 'Do not think that I have come to abolish the Law or the Prophets' (Matt. 5:17), and from there moves to the observation that the Pharisees have set the standards *too low* to be valid for being Kingdom people.

We are back to our question: 'So how do you do better than a Pharisee?' Jesus demonstrates the answer in a series of 'You have heard that it is said . . . but I say' comparisons. What the Pharisees said is righteousness is exceeded by what Jesus says is recognised as Kingdom righteousness. Each of the actions Jesus describes can be traced back to the be-like-your-Father values set out in the Beatitudes.

The righteousness that Jesus speaks of is the righteousness that flows out of the values that Kingdom-type people cherish. I think the *Clear Word* paraphrase of this verse says it well: 'I tell you with absolute certainty that you cannot do everything the scribes and Pharisees tell you and live the way they do and expect to get to heaven. Unless your life is guided by higher values than theirs, you can have no part in God's kingdom.'

The higher values cluster around that core value that describes the essential character of God – love. When the Kingdom citizen acts out of love, he or she is demonstrating the righteousness that exceeds. Thus Ellen White writes: '. . . it is love alone which in the sight of Heaven makes any act of value. Whatever is done from love, however small it may appear in the estimation of men, is accepted and rewarded of God.' (*The Great Controversy*, page 487.)

When our deacons, pastors and other members act towards others out of the values of, for example, Sabbath-keeping, dress standards, veganism, tithing or any other standard of righteousness apart from love, they demonstrate that they are not sons or daughters of the King. Their DNA needs changing.

The scary thing is that when we act in this way we have become darkness, not light, and salt that has lost its savour. We betray the Kingdom of God. We have joined another father rather than our heavenly Father.

Chapter 12

Proactive and reactive people

There are two kinds of people in the world. They are described in the well-known line – 'Two men looked out through prison bars;
One saw mud, the other saw stars.'

This raises some important questions. Why did one see mud and the other, stars? And which are you most like?

Someone else argued that the two kinds of people in the world can be recognised in their use of just three words – God, morning and good. One wakes up and says, 'Good morning God!' while the other awakes with the words, 'Good God – morning!'

Which are you?

Stephen Covey argues that those people who are driven by the situation they are in – their environment, or immediate context – are reactive people: They are people who tend to see mud. Those people who subject their outward conditions to their inner values are proactive people, and they tend to see stars.

The reactive person allows what happens to them to create their response. Proactive people respond to what happens to them from the values they hold.

Covey goes on to argue that the ability to *subordinate an impulse* to a value is the essence of the proactive person.

George Bernard Shaw contributes to our point in the following quotation: 'The reasonable man adapts himself to the conditions that surround him. The unreasonable man adapts the surrounding conditions to himself.' Then he adds that ' . . . all progress depends on the unreasonable man.'

I walked into a shop some years ago with my wife. We entered through doors that closed themselves by means of a tension bar. We had walked about 5 metres into the store when a sales lady standing behind the counter chatting with two other colleagues called to me. 'Hey,' she called, 'close the door!' I was surprised that she called me, and, looking in the direction she was pointing, saw that one of the two doors we had entered through had only partially closed. The closing mechanism must have been faulty. I thought for a moment about whose responsibility the door was, but then walked back and closed it. Returning to my wife I simply said, 'You can look at anything you want in this shop but I will not buy it!'

Why did the lady do that? Was it her intention to stop us buying or to lose a customer? Was it that she valued closed doors because they kept the cold out? Or maybe that is how she usually spoke to her kids running through the home: 'Hey, close the door!' I wonder how she may have responded if a highly respected member of the community – say, the Mayor – had walked through the door? Whatever the reason or value she held – it was not the value of good service. I am sure service was some sort of value, but here it was either a reactive or situational (depends who comes through the door) value, or simply not high on her list of values. It was not an embedded, proactive value.

Which are you – a proactive or reactive person? Are the values in your life intentionally built in, thus making you a proactive person, or are the values there, but not really clearly worked out, thus making you a reactive person? Stories such as those in the fourth chapter of this book challenge us to ask questions about what values those deacons had and whether their values, like dress standards, etc, are more important than winning a person to Christ or exhibiting the fragrant beauty of a Christ-like life.

When the issues are carefully thought about, it becomes clear that deacons such as those in the stories above have not intentionally worked out the values that exceed. They are, as Covey writes, 'reactive people driven by feelings, by circumstances, by conditions, by their environment' (*The Seven Habits of Highly Effective People*, page 72). I would add that they are driven by their immediate priorities, by who it is they are talking to, by the value that happens to hold their thinking at that moment. They should be, as Covey again writes, 'proactive people . . . driven by values – carefully thought about, selected, and internalised values' (ibid.).

This is easier said than done.

How is your commitment to Christian values? How would you come out in the Princeton Good Samaritan test?

Some years ago two Princeton University psychologists – John Darley and Daniel Batson – went to Princeton Theological Seminary and conducted an experiment based on the story of the Good Samaritan. Keep in mind that the people in the experiment were seminarians. They were at a prestigious theology school training for ministry. These are the kind of people in whom we would expect to find Kingdom values: if not embedded, at least given strong assent to.

The psychologists divided the students into two groups. Each group was to make a short presentation, ostensibly as part of their training. One group was assigned the topic 'The Good Samaritan', while the other group's topic was 'The Value of Professional Ministry to Religious Life'. On the day of the exam, each student was individually told just before the exam when they were due for their presentation. There was a difference – half of the two groups were told that they had to go to the venue immediately as the examiners were waiting for them, while the other half were told that there was plenty of time to get to the venue. To get to the room each person had to go along a certain path. On the path Darley and Batson had planted an actor pretending to be an injured man, groaning for help. This is why the experiment was named the Princeton Good Samaritan test. Who stopped? It seems the presentation topic made no difference. The only thing that mattered was whether the student was in a rush. Of the group that were, 10% stopped to help. Of the group who knew they had time to spare, 63% stopped.

Darley and Batson concluded that the convictions of your heart and the actual contents of your thoughts are less important, in the end, in guiding your actions than the immediate context of your behaviour. The words, 'Oh, you're late' had the effect of making someone who was ordinarily compassionate into someone who was indifferent to suffering; of turning someone, in that particular moment, into a different person (Malcolm Gladwell, *The Tipping Point*, page 166).

If we are to build churches that rightly represent the Kingdom of Heaven, then we must be proactive in what we say. We must do this individually and as organisations. We must define what the values of the Kingdom are: those values that 'exceed' (as Jesus put it). We must state them, embrace them, be accountable to them and intentionally build them into the DNA of our hearts and organisations.

Chapter 13

Don't be deceived

I once had a young pastor in our ministry team who was a brilliant mimic. At pastors' meetings, without saying a word, he would set the whole team off giggling except the person who he was mimicking. The person being mimicked just couldn't see what the rest were laughing about. I often wondered, when the team laughed without my being aware of what they were laughing at, whether I was the victim this time. There were occasions when I had to tell him to stop it before someone recognised that they were the target and got upset with him. I probably needn't have feared for him, because we humans have a very difficult time seeing the truth about ourselves.

It is a part of the problem of the 'log' in the eye that we referred to in the previous chapter, but we need to take this a little further. We not only find it easy to see others' faults and not our own, but we are also prone to deceiving ourselves that our 'faults' are not really faults, or that those of others are worse than ours.

The little book *Leadership and Self-deception* (by the Arbinger Trust) has three illustrations that help to explain this phenomenon.

The first refers to a man getting onto a flight where the

seating is open and he knows there are a few spare seats. He decides that he would like to have the space and luxury of having one of these spare seats next to him. So he grabs a window seat and places some stuff on the next seat, spreads himself wide and opens his newspaper across both seats. Every now and then he peeps over the paper to see if anyone is coming down the aisle and possibly eyeing the empty seat. If he suspects so the paper spreads even wider and the message is clearly sent – do not even think about this seat – find another one! In moments the thought of the luxury of having the adjacent seat free moves from being a desire to being something he deserves. After all, he is tired and wants the space to relax; there are other seats and he has had a hard day; he needs peace and quiet, and his own space. And that thinking creates an enemy of the person looking for a seat. He or she has suddenly become thoughtless, unattractive, uncaring, a nuisance and a threat or even the enemy – all because the man is only seeing things from his perspective. He is in his box. He has deceived himself.

The second story has a couple boarding a flight but somehow they were not able to book their seats together. Again they are informed that the flight has one or two free seats and the hostess hopes to find someone willing to exchange seats and offer them two seats together. As they are standing there a lady steps out from where she is seated and says, 'The seat next to me is free: why don't I take one of your tickets and you take these two seats?'

What is the difference between the two stories? In the first, the man is in his box and can only see his needs; in the second, the lady is thinking outside of the box and can see the needs of others. But it is more than that. The man in the box has not only become obsessed with his needs or wants, but he has deceived himself into attributing evil intent to the other passenger.

A third illustration can explain further. Here a couple are asleep in their bed when their baby begins to cry. The husband wakes immediately and thinks, 'I need to jump up and hush the baby before it wakes my darling wife.' But the bed is so comfortable and the baby stutters a little as if it may soon stop crying. The husband settles back in hope. Then the baby continues to cry and now the husband's thinking goes like this: 'My wife must have woken by now. Why is she not seeing to the baby? She must be expecting me to do it! But she knows I have to get up early to go to work and she can always nap during the day when the baby sleeps.' This logic can go as far as picturing what was at first the darling wife, now as the lazy, selfish wife. The man began out of his box, then got into his box, and is now experiencing the phenomenon of self-deception.

The Kingdom values-led person lives outside of the box because he or she lives by the values that exceed and is always seeking to be other-centred. The scribe or Pharisee lives in their box. It is a box in which they can only see their own needs and from where they can go about deceiving themselves – justifying their attitudes and actions and attributing evil to the other person.

Being in the box not only makes a person blind to the needs of others but leads him or her to attribute negative intentions to them as well. This can in turn lead to a negative reaction towards the person and a subsequent cycle of negative responses that simply confirm the opinion of the person in the box.

The challenge for the values-led person is to live a discipled-to-the-values life.

The following may be helpful.

- Don't think you can be perfect. Plead for and earnestly desire the other-centredness of Christ. Let Christ in you be the key to living Kingdom values.

- Be humble. Take time to reflect on incidents that occur and ask yourself if you were *in the box* during the incident.

- If you find that you were in your box – smile about the grace of God towards your weakness and apologise freely, remembering that we all struggle to stay out of the box.

- Resist totally the temptation to see or point out other people's 'box behaviour'. Don't become the Pharisee pointing out the eye specks of others. Let your values-led life be the sermon. Should someone ask you about your values, share with them humbly and honestly about yourself and point them to God's help.

- Don't become discouraged when you find yourself back in your box. Seek the encouragement of the Lord Jesus to fight the good fight, as did the apostle Paul – read 1 Corinthians 9:24-27.

- Keep in mind that God delights in the values of His Kingdom, which He is embedding in you, and that He gives grace and more grace to His children as they seek to be like Him.

Chapter 14

All change!

Why are some people unfaithful? Erick Janssen of the Kinsey Institute (*The Change Book* by M. Krogerus & R. Tschappeler, page 44) has developed an infidelity matrix in which he uses the analogy of the accelerator and brake pedals to describe a person's responses to sexual urges and to faithfulness. We all have access to the drive accelerator or gas pedal and the braking power of choice. The gas pedal represents our passion, but the faithful person knows how to use the brakes. Janssen's conclusion is that the faithful person knows how to promise undying love-fuel to one person – over and over again.

Being values-led is analogous. It is not just a matter of choosing some good values and practising them. It is a matter of choosing all the 'exceed' values of the Kingdom of Heaven and discipling oneself to *those* values over and over again. And that's part of what makes it so hard and yet, in a certain sense, also easy.

The easy part is that the beauty and harmony, the mercy and justice, the grace and truth of the Kingdom values make the laws of that Kingdom so attractive that it is obvious that that's the Way! I believe it resonates with the image of God within each of us.

The difficult part is that this Kingdom is ultimately a denial of so much that we are. It goes contrary to what is the normal default of our sinful nature – self-centredness. This makes it difficult because the process of growing into that new creature that comes with the new birth is a now-and-not-yet experience. It requires a daily struggle of submitting my heart and mind to the rule of Christ. It involves a putting on of the mind of Christ, of daily taking up the cross, of choosing servanthood, of submitting my body and self to the law of Christ – over and over again.

In my personal experience I am amazed and humbled when someone purports to see Christ in me, for my eyes see more and more the depth of the depravity in me while at the same time an increasing adoration of the character and kingdom of Jesus Christ. I understand the importance of morning and evening prayers, but far more I recognise the vital role of praying without ceasing – discipling myself to ask which values are determining my moment-by-moment interactions and relationships.

Thus being Kingdom values-led requires a change to, as well as a choice of, those values – over and over again.

Jesus spoke of people who are experts at seeing the speck in other people's eyes while ignoring the beam in their own. Well, a speck is a speck, and the person with the speck would do better with it removed. The expert with the 4x3-inch plank sees the speck clearly but is going to do great damage as they swing that plank across the face of the patient. Jesus' advice is that the expert remove the plank first – and this is the hard part again. We become comfortable with our 'eye logs' and expert at seeing the 'specks' in others. Becoming values-led involves the difficult process of recognising and removing our logs, and then learning to minister to the specs of others with understanding, compassion and grace – Kingdom values.

Brian McClaren uses an illustration that is helpful and which I will bend herein for my purposes.

Three circles describe what is important in our spiritual concerns.

The first and largest circle represents me and my spirituality. I will use this to represent the Adventist who makes it their priority to be ready for the coming of the Lord Jesus. Their lives are focused on their spiritual preparation. They study their Sabbath lessons well, they have their daily devotions, they attend all the meetings at church that they can. Their diet is vegetarian, if not vegan. They are careful to guard their ears and eyes from the lust and evil that surround them. Their ideal is a home in the country where they can be close to God and away from evil influences that may distract them from their goal – to be ready when Jesus comes. After all – isn't that the point of Adventism?

The second circle represents the next most important matter in their lives. It represents church. Church and attending it are important in that the whole purpose of it is to get us ready for the coming of Jesus and then heaven. I reserve my best clothes for church and guard the edges of the Sabbath well. Church is like the Temple of old – it is a sacred place – where only that which is holy must be allowed. I go there to further my spirituality – to be confirmed in my views during Sabbath School classes and have them affirmed by the sermons. After all, church is there to prepare me for the coming of Jesus. I don't particularly bother how outsiders or visitors may feel about my church as long as I am comfortable there.

Finally, there is that small circle. This represents the world and all that is in it. It is full of evil. It is a lost world, driven by the passions of lust, greed and arrogance (1 John 2:16). It is best that we have as little to do with it as possible. It is the enemy of our spiritual preparation for the second coming of Jesus.

> Our big concern is getting 'me' to heaven;
> the church is a help but often a mess; and
> the world is hopeless!

But let us consider a reordering of those priorities.

Let us begin with the most important priority circle again. This time what is most important to me is the world. I mean this in the sense that God did when John wrote: 'God so loved the world . . .'

What if our big concern were the world – not to *escape* it, but to reach it for Christ. What if those lost people out in the world were to become our number-one priority? What if our energies were to become focused like those of the woman, shepherd or father searching for their lost coin, sheep or son in Luke 15?

And what if the church were to become our way of collectively helping the world? Our priority here would be that the church be attractive and comfortable *to lost people* rather than *to me* in my aim to meet Jesus. My contribution to the church and concern for it would then be so that it could help the world, wouldn't it? As for me and my preparation for the advent – somehow that becomes secondary so that we might save others. Here the grace of God to me and our faith in the salvation He gives us come to the fore, rather than that which I might accomplish to make myself ready.

It may be that my analogy above makes the mistake of creating an unbiblical separation of love and hatred of the world. A scriptural case could be argued for both positions. Our Gospel is both *world-denying* and *world-affirming*. We are to be in but not of the world. We are both to go into all the world as well as to flee from it. But I would like to make the case that so many of our values are fashioned by the culture of the first order of circles, where our preparation for heaven prioritises the values we are led by. They are values that are critical of the world and affirming of God's love to ourselves. This approach is all about me and my salvation: whereas the second order would find us being far more Christ-like when we as individuals and church organisations are focused on saving the lost. Here the approach is all about the lost and their salvation. Here the values are critical of ourselves and affirming of God's love to the world.

Being other-centred is the essential value of the Kingdom. Thus, being Kingdom values-led is a reversal of the values surrounding the spiritual preparation approach. It is not an easy road, for it involves denying myself and loving my enemies. But as long as 'this train is bound for heaven' and 'don't carry nothing but the good and holy' – or, as one version has it . . .

'This train don't count no jokers,

no bad women nor the cigarette smokers' –

I would submit that it is going the wrong way. Values-leading calls out, 'All change!' We all need to get off our comfortable ride to heaven and understand that spirituality or strength to resist being unfaithful is best gained when we are engaged, over and over again, in aggressive service to others.

As Ellen White penned in *The Acts of the Apostles*, page 105, 'The persecution that came upon the church in Jerusalem resulted in giving a great impetus to the work of the gospel. Success had attended the ministry of the word in that place, and there was danger that the disciples would linger there too long, unmindful of the Saviour's commission to go to all the world. Forgetting that **strength to resist evil is best gained by aggressive service**, they began to think that they had no work so important as that of shielding the church in Jerusalem from the attacks of the enemy. Instead of educating the new converts to carry the gospel to those who had not heard it, they were in danger of taking a course that would lead all to be satisfied with what had been accomplished. To scatter His representatives abroad, where they could work for others, God permitted persecution to come upon them. Driven from Jerusalem, the believers "went everywhere preaching the word." '

Chapter 15

Aspirational and actual values

Working out one's values – whether they be held by an individual or an organisation – is simple. It doesn't take rocket science to figure out that values like mercy, excellence, service, humility, purity, truthfulness, etc, are great values. The problem isn't knowing what the values are; the problem is in practising them. In other words, we can aspire to a list of values, but neglect them while we are busy actually living out another set of values. That second but actual list of values can be good values in themselves – they are just easier to keep and have within them the ability to kid us that we are doing well. We are talking here about the difference between aspirational and actual values.

Jesus puts His finger on an example of actual and aspirational values in one of His strong attacks on the values of the church leaders of His day.

'Woe to you, scribes and Pharisees, hypocrites! For you tithe mint and dill and cumin, and have neglected the weightier matters of the law: justice and mercy and faithfulness. These you ought to have done, without neglecting the others.' (Matt. 23:23.)

Things to note about this verse:

First, the passionate strength of His criticism. 'Woe!' His use of this word carries with it undertones of a judgement threat. It took my mind to His strong statement that 'never' or 'in no case' can one 'enter into the kingdom of heaven' with such values (Matt. 5:20, ESV and KJV).

Second, there is the value of faithful tithing. Any treasurer or stewardship leader will tell you that that is a good value. Jesus in fact commends them when He says, 'These you ought to have done. . . .'

How is it, then, that a person so faithful in tithing comes under His threat of judgement?

The answer is that while these scribes and Pharisees would have agreed that 'justice and mercy and faithfulness' are good values, by their 'neglected' (past) and 'neglecting' (present) actions they demonstrated what their highest values were. The 'weightier', aspirational values were ignored in favour of their exacting, purposeful practising of lighter values.

This is what the deacon was doing when he sent the visitor home to dress appropriately before coming to church. The deacon subscribed to a good value – dress standards. I wonder how exactly the deacon had his standards of dress worked out. How many inches or even millimetres should a dress be from the ground, ankle or below (of course) the knee? This could make an interesting discussion, but one has to ask: 'What has happened to mercy or the desire to win lost people or grace?' Our deacon had neglected the 'weightier matters of the law'.

Ask that deacon whether he values lost people, mercy and grace, and he will say, 'Of course I value those!' But he has become so focused on majoring in the minor values (important as they are) that the 'weightier matters' have fallen off the scale completely.

Aspirational values are values that we say we believe in or hold to but never do, while actual values are the values we practise. Holding values and not doing them adds up to being a hypocrite. That's why our 'mint and dill and cumin' tithe-paying friend, who neglects the values of 'justice, mercy and faithfulness', comes under the threat of Jesus' judgement. 'Woe to you . . . hypocrites!'

So what is our deacon meant to do?

He must sit down and make a list of values that belong to or should characterise Kingdom people or organisations – like churches. What are those weightier matters of the law? A read through the Sermon on the Mount in Matthew 5-7 would be a good starter. Other passages worth reading might include 1 Corinthians 13, Galatians 5:22-23, Micah 6:6-8 and Romans 12:9-21. Then list the values that are found there. Add to that list the other values that we hold dear but that may be not so prominent in the Scriptures, or may even be absent from them – dress and health standards, reading and entertainment values, etc. Then categorise them into 'important but lighter' and 'important but weightier' sets of values. It may be helpful to do this with a few other people to make sure we are being fair in our evaluations of the values of the Kingdom. Another excellent test of a 'weightier' value is whether you can find a story in the gospels showing that it was an important value to Jesus. Keep in mind, too, that the scale of values that the Pharisees held was completely unacceptable to Him.

The 'weightier' values that you arrive at should be our aspirational values. Now our task is to make them our actual values. Working out whether our values are aspirational or actual is a matter of asking ourselves some hard questions.

For example, if one of your aspirational values is to spend time with the Lord, ask yourself how many hours you spent with Him during the past two or three days, or even the past week. If the answer is none or just a few minutes, then you can be sure it is still only an aspirational value, not an actual value.

If another of your aspirational values is lost people, ask yourself when you last talked to a 'lost' person about serious matters or anything at all. If the answer is, 'Hmmm, last year,' 'last month' or, 'I can't remember,' then it is definitely an aspirational value.

If grace is one of your values, ask yourself when you last performed a random act of grace? If the value is helping the poor, ask yourself how you relate to homeless people you pass in the street.

Becoming actual in our aspirational values is not easy. It requires an understanding of our overwhelming indebtedness to grace (Matthew 18:21-35), an outpouring of the fruits of the Spirit into our hearts (Romans 5:5) and a commitment to purposefully embed these values into our daily living.

Most of Jesus' conflicts with the Pharisees were over the issue of their hypocrisy. Unfortunately, their aspirational values had been replaced by their actual values. That is why Jesus taught, 'So do and observe whatever they tell you, but not the works they do. For they preach, but do not practise.' (Matt. 23:3.) They were so focused by their actual values that they could not see the greater values that represented the Kingdom of Heaven.

Some years ago I pastored a church located in an area that was a tough place to work. The building was often broken into and the members were often harassed by local youth in the street. One of their tactics that really got to me was when they would walk very closely behind my wife and me, then spit on her back. When we turned around they would say, 'What? I didn't do anything.'

Late one evening I had to get something from the church. There was a low wall in the front and a teen was sitting on it. As I walked past he swore a list of expletives at me. I ignored him (as usual) and went into the church, fuming. I thought I was over the anger when I came out, however, and walked past him again. Again he cussed me using strong expletives. I should have walked on, but something in me snapped and I grabbed him by the collar of his jacket and pushed him over the wall, onto his back. I then pushed my fist into his mouth and told him that if he spoke like that to me again I would punch his mouth in.

As I walked away I went into conflict mode – not with the lad, but with my values. My higher aspirational values told me to go back, apologise and treat him with grace. A lower, actual value, however, said that he needed to be taught to show me respect. It took three days of wrestling with my core value. I even found the street social worker and asked what his advice was: to which he replied, 'You should have punched him. That's the only way to get respect.'

I eventually overcame my pride (a big issue in keeping to higher values), found him and apologised, promising him that no matter what expletives he used when speaking to me, I would never treat him like that again. We became friends, he never swore at me again and years later when we ran into each other again he greeted me like a long-lost friend.

I love this anecdote involving Herb Kelleher, who was at the time CEO of Southwest Airlines, a company that holds very strongly to its values – one of which is adding fun to customers' journeys. Mr Kelleher got a letter from a customer complaining of inappropriate humour being used by stewards when making announcements. It is understood that the announcement was something like, 'In the event of landing on water we will distribute towels and cocktails.'

Most CEOs would have replied with an apology and assurance that flight staff would be told to be more careful. Not Kelleher. His reply was short and simple – 'Dear Sir, We'll miss you!' The point was that the company's values are actual and would not be compromised or changed for lesser ones.

Jesus, similarly, never compromised on His commitment to the core values of grace and mercy. On a number of occasions when the religious leaders tried to make Him conform to their values or rules for religious practice, Jesus countered that God desired 'mercy, and not sacrifice' to be our embedded and practised, actual core value (see Matthew 9:13 and 12:7).

Chapter 16

Being values-led is not easy!

Manfred Kets de Vries, in his book *Reflections on Groups and Organizations* (Jossey Bass, 2011), relates the following story: 'The lion was completely convinced about his dominance of the animal kingdom. One day he wanted to check whether all the other animals knew he was the undisputed king of the jungle. He was so confident that he decided not to talk to the small creatures. Instead he went straight to the bear: "Who is the king of the jungle?" asked the lion. The bear replied, "Of course, no one else but you, sir!" to which the lion gave a great roar of approval.

'He continued his journey and met the tiger. "Who is the king of the jungle?" The tiger quickly responded, "All of us know that you are the king." The lion gave another roar of pleasure. Next on his list was the elephant. He caught up with the elephant at the edge of the river and asked the same question, "Who is the king of the jungle?" The elephant trumpeted, lifted his trunk, grabbed the lion, threw him into the air and smashed him into a tree. He fished him out of the tree and pounded him into the ground, lifted him up once more and dumped him into the river. Then he jumped on top of the lion, dragged him through the mud, and finally left him hanging in some bushes.

'The lion, dirty, beaten, bruised, and battered, struggled to get to his feet. He looked the elephant sadly in the eyes and said, "Look, just because you don't know the answer, there's no reason for you to be so mean-spirited about it." '

De Vries' point is that leaders and organisations find it difficult to change; nor is change an easy and painless process.

This story is told about the pastor of a rural church. The geography of the area was rolling farmland dotted here and there with long-established farmsteads. The church was made up of families who had worked their farms for many years. But change marches on and the city began to invade the countryside, with city folk beginning to build little mansions here and there between the farms. The church began to grow too, with an influx of visitors. The pastor was delighted; the pews were filling, as was the offering plate, and so he called his diaconate together to train them.

He prepared a page of instructions on how to welcome new people. In the middle of his presentation, one of the deacons crumpled up the paper, threw it on the floor and said, 'Pastor, I don't want these new people in our church! They come in here as if they own the place, sit where they want to and have no respect for our family pews; their children are noisy and just spend their time playing on their pads or whatever they call them!' The meeting ends with many agreeing with the deacon, and the hapless pastor is left dumbfounded.

He contacts his mentor. After listening to the story the mentor explains that the pastor has erred in seeking to implement *tactical* change, whereas he needs to begin with *transformational* change.

What he needed to do was to take his church through a process of going back to basics, asking the questions that will explore the purposes of the church and the reason Christ called His church into existence. This exploration of the values of the Kingdom of Christ will challenge and possibly rebuke the culture of that country church, and that is why the process is not easy. To not undertake that process is to guarantee the demise of His church and its replacement by new churches that will meet the needs of the changing environment.

Change is difficult because it is transformational and not just tactical. Tactical change without transformational change may involve an outward change of actions, but, where the heart of the individual or organisation is not transformed, those actions will be reluctantly done, with no synergy between the inner motive and the outward action. Becoming values-led is a process of aligning the heart with the values of the Kingdom, and that process can be very challenging.

In the introduction of this book I refer to my experience when, in a class on leadership, we were required to reflectively create a list of personal values. I thought that this would be an easy task. All I needed to do was write up some values that had a biblical basis and the task would be done. I drew up my list, and was pleased with them, but when I took time to reflect on them I soon discovered that there were some that did not describe my normal behaviour. One that particularly challenged me was the need to be humble and value criticism. While seeing that valuing criticism inevitably ended in a win-win result because it built relationships and taught me to do things better, and was therefore to be valued, I found that my default response to criticism was to become defensive. Humility was only an aspirational value, not an actual value. My ultimate denial of the value of biblical humility dawned on me when I found myself considering its removal from my list. Fortunately the value is still on my list today, but I have had to work hard at disciplines and strategies that help me to be accountable for implementing and practising it.

That's why being values-led is not easy. We have within our human natures a propensity to get back into our boxes (see Chapter 13) and so there is a daily struggle to 'cross out' that nature and replace it with the mind of Christ. I admit to often either smiling at myself or seeing the need of prayer when I catch my pride kicking against that value. Then I must remind myself that the recalibrating of my values is the work of sanctification, which is the work of a lifetime.

Another reason why being values-led is not easy is because values are principles, rather than descriptions of actions or tactics. Thus, values will always be aspirational, because they are eternal principles that constantly need temporal reapplication in our ever-changing world. Sadly, some Christians think that *some of the applications are the value itself*, rather than recognising that the application of a specific value may actually vary from context to context, or between different cultures and persons.

De Vries works with corporations that seek to do value change. He claims that such change requires a minimum of three 5-day courses separated by as much as seven weeks between each one. During that process there is much reflection, heart searching, recognitions of failure, public disclosure, rebuilding of trust relationships, etc.

Being values-led is not easy and the church that assumes it can be done at one board meeting is naïve.

Screwtape* offers a helpful image on embedding virtues:

'Think of your man as a series of concentric circles, his will being the innermost, his intellect coming next, and finally his fantasy. You can hardly hope, at once, to exclude from all the circles everything that smells of the Enemy: but you must keep on shoving all the virtues outward till they are finally located in the circle of fantasy, and all the desirable qualities inward into the will. It is only insofar as they reach the will and are there embodied in habits that the virtues are really fatal to us. (I don't, of course, mean what the patient mistakes for his will, the conscious fume and fret of resolutions and clenched teeth, but the real centre, what the Enemy calls the Heart.) All sorts of virtues painted in the fantasy or approved by the intellect or even, in some measure, loved and admired, will not keep a man from Our Father's house: indeed they may make him more amusing when he gets there.'

(From *The Screwtape Letters*, by C. S. Lewis.)

The apostle Paul understood the difficulty of embedding a core value in the 'flesh' where 'sin' dwells. See Romans 7:18-25:

'For I know that nothing good dwells in me, that is, in my flesh. For I have the desire to do what is right, but not the ability to carry it out. For I do not do the good I want, but the evil I do not want is what I keep on doing. Now if I do what I do not want, it is no longer I who do it, but sin that dwells within me.

'So I find it to be a law that when I want to do right, evil lies close at hand. For I delight in the law of God, in my inner being, but I see in my members another law waging war against the law of my mind and making me captive to the law of sin that dwells in my members. Wretched man that I am! Who will deliver me from this body of death? Thanks be to God through Jesus Christ our Lord! So then, I myself serve the law of God with my mind, but with my flesh I serve the law of sin.'

It requires the 'deliverance' of Jesus, a determination to serve the law with the mind and the prayerful persistence Jesus taught in the story of the widow of Luke 18:1-8 and the friends of Luke 11:5-8. As Alden Thompson says in his Sabbath School lesson commentary of 9 August 2014, '. . . each parable does teach a simple truth about prayer: Stay with it! Apparently there is something about persistent prayer that transforms the one who prays.'

Maybe this is hardest when relaxing at home – like when David sinned with Bathsheba – or in the unguarded moments of conflict with brethren at church.

It requires us to march to a different drumbeat, one that belongs to another Kingdom. It requires us to remain true to dream the impossible dream. Living a values-led life may appear somewhat quixotic – chasing 'exceed' values regardless of material or other interests, sometimes in the face of scorn – but it is a dream worth living.

'To dream the impossible dream
To fight the unbeatable foe
To bear with unbearable sorrow
To run where the brave dare not go

'To right the unrightable wrong
To love pure and chaste from afar
To try when your arms are too weary
To reach the unreachable star

'This is my quest
To follow that star
No matter how hopeless
No matter how far

'To fight for the right
Without question or pause
To be willing to march into hell
For a heavenly cause

'And I know if I'll only be true
To this glorious quest
That my heart will lie peaceful and calm
When I'm laid to my rest

'And the world will be better for this
That one man, scorned and covered with scars
Still strove with his last ounce of courage
To reach the unreachable star'

'The Impossible Dream (The Quest)', lyrics by Joe Darion

The Screwtape Letters are a fictional series of correspondence purporting to be advice from a senior devil to one of his young assistants. They were written by Clive Staples Lewis, a committed Christian, in an attempt to demonstrate how vulnerable Christians may be to temptation.

Chapter 17

What values can do for your church

O K – what's in it for us? Aubrey Malphurs (*Values-driven Leadership*) and Jim Kouzes and Barry Posner (*The Leadership Challenge*) are the experts on this. Allow me to share with you from what they say.

1. Values define what your ministry is.
Your essential or core values, clearly defined, help your congregation or team to understand who you are and what you stand for. Your values will define not only what you do (your strategy), but how you do it (your methods), and will also affect the appearance of your building and places of worship and ministry. The culture that you are, or your church is, is defined and shaped by your core values.

2. Your values spell out what is important – what you have got to do.
In the early church the apostles faced a crisis when there was an argument over the distribution of food and accusations of discrimination. The story is there in Acts 6:1-7. It was an important crisis, and the apostles could easily have decided that this needed their direct

and personal action: but, rather than getting side-tracked from the very important to the important, they assigned the matter to several others and spelt out the values that they had to focus on – the values of prayer and the ministry of the Word. In other words, their primary values determined the vision they had and what they needed to do.

3. Values invite personal involvement.

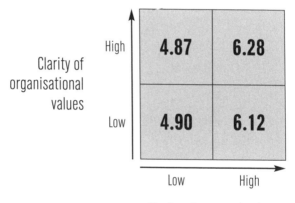

Clarity of organisational values

	High	4.87	6.28
	Low	4.90	6.12
		Low	High

Clarity of personal values

A study referred to by Kouzes and Posner tracks responses to how employees are affected by the individual and the organisation having clear values. The scores are out of 7.

The first box, with 4.90 in it, measures the level of commitment by the individual to the organisation. In this category, neither the organisation nor the employee have clear values. The message that may come to the employee is that the organisation does not particularly care about anything (including the employee), and the employee's response is, 'Well, I don't care either!'

The 4.87 box is where the organisation has clear values but the individual does not have clear values. At first sight it appears strange that the level of commitment drops. The researchers argue that this is because the individual reacts to the disconnect between his lack of values and the clarity of the organisation's values. The employee may feel a little uncomfortable with such a focused organisation. Give him or her time!

The 6.12 box is where the individual already has clear values but the organisation does not. Here is the proactive employee, a person of integrity who has worked out their core values and is committed to them. Such individuals will commit themselves to whatever organisations they join. Joseph and Daniel come to mind, as examples of individuals who became high achievers in organisations that lacked clear values.

The 6.28 box is where the individual and organisation are both clear about and committed to the same values. This is where the highest level of commitment is achieved.

The bottom line of the study is that the people who have the greatest clarity about both personal and organisational values will show the highest degree of commitment to the organisation.

The lesson for us is that values clearly stated and clearly taught promote loyalty, invite participation and close the back door of the organisation. They invite people at a heart level, who have experienced the world and its superficial values, to want to be a part of such an organisation or environment. Like when you take a seat in a highly comfortable chair or car, or visit an organisation that practises excellence, your inner man says, 'I like this.' It is a positive 'chemistry' that we sense.

Places where the organisation and staff, or members, have and share clear values experience the highest staff loyalty, involvement and retention rates in their particular industry. (More of this in Chapter 20, where we touch on lessons from the Ritz-Carlton organisation.)

4. Values embrace positive change.

We live in a time of constant and rapid change. What do we embrace? What do we reject? Shall we use screens and projectors or not? Are there meetings where guitars and drums could be permitted or not? As long as the building, times of meetings, organ music, platform dress style, traditional order of services, and so on, are the sacred cows of our churches, change will always be a difficult struggle.

Values provide a moral GPS (global positioning system) to guide our decisions so that we can embrace positive change. Establishing not only our vision, but the values underlying that vision, provide that moral guidance. The only sacred cows that should rightfully guide our decisions are our core scriptural doctrines or beliefs, our vision and our values. The question that should guide our changes is, 'Does the change agree with or contradict the core values and vision of this organisation?' Having clear values helps us embrace positive change.

This does not mean that other things that are valued – like what we eat or how we dress or what we do on Sabbath, and so on – are to be ignored. As Jesus said of the less important values of the scribes and Pharisees – '. . . For you tithe mint and rue and every herb, and neglect justice and the love of God. These you ought to have done, without neglecting the others.' (Luke 11:42.)

5. Values influence overall behaviour.

Values determine, or at least specify, what our behaviours should be.

It was Augustine who stated, 'Love God and do whatever you please. . . .' At first the quotation may feel like licence to have any standard of behaviour: but when love for God is more than an aspirational concept, but rather an actual, life-embedded value, then, as Paul says in 2 Corinthians 5:14, '. . . the love of Christ controls us.' Augustine's quotation in full is, 'Love God and do whatever you please: for the soul trained in love to God will do nothing to offend the One who is Beloved.'[1]

When you and your church embed a value like 'love' into the heart of your culture it will influence the overall behaviour of that culture, just as surely as the 'self-centredness' value of much of secular society permeates and influences all its behaviour.

The wise man wrote of this a long time ago in Proverbs 4:23 (KJV): 'Keep thy heart with all diligence; for out of it are the issues of life.'

The heart's values, unexamined or examined, are the basis of all our behaviours. They determine what we will or will not do. Thus our values must be what we 'do' first. Before vision, policies, goals or standards come values, and they must determine what comes next.

6. Values inspire people to action.

The phenomenon called volunteerism generally occurs because of values. What gets a member to step up to serve in the programmes of their church is when they see that those programmes tie in with the values it espouses and that the member loves.

There is no doubt that our hearts often resonate with lofty ideals, and it is those heroes of the values of the Kingdom that inspire us to follow suit. When people state that they love their church - and we wish we heard this more - it is because they are attracted to the great values that the church stands for. For this they will give their best efforts - often their lives. We were created for the highest dreams, as Joe Darion wrote:

'To fight for the right without question or pause: To be willing to march into hell for a heavenly cause.'

Biblical values infuse people with meaning and direction in life. And to be energised to action in a church that holds inspiring values means that our members commit themselves to the body of Christ, thereby experiencing authentic biblical community.

7. Values enhance credible leadership.

Brene Brown, in her book *Daring Greatly*, argues that the greatest threat to creativity, innovation and learning in any organisation is the disengagement of people from those organisations because of a disconnect that arises between their leaders and the values they preach. She writes: 'The space between our practised values (what we're actually doing, thinking and feeling) and our aspirational values (what we want to do, think, and feel) is the value gap, or what I call 'the disengagement divide'. It's where we lose our employees, our clients, our students, our teachers, our congregations, and even our children.'

When Christian leaders authentically own and model the values of the Kingdom, they enhance their credibility and by their lives call people to accept those very values. Peter Drucker writes: '. . . if [the manager] lacks in character and integrity – no matter how knowledgeable, how brilliant, how successful – he destroys. He destroys people, the most valuable resource of the enterprise. He destroys spirit. And he destroys performance.'

Such a person betrays the King and His Kingdom and will destroy the trust of the members in that Kingdom.

8. Values contribute to ministry success.

If you combine the seven benefits of values outlined above it becomes obvious that values contribute to success in ministry. Imagine that your church knows what is important; that its leaders model the Kingdom; and that its members are loyal and willing to step up to serve! People commit themselves to values that inspire them; they will serve harder, have more enthusiasm, more pride, and will delight in the colleague striving to serve the same values and work longer for great causes. They are also more likely to be creative and risk-taking in serving the Kingdom.

Notice how the value of grace affected the apostle Paul: '. . . by the grace of God I am what I am, and his grace towards me was not in vain. On the contrary, I worked harder than any of them, though it was not I, but the grace of God that is with me' (1 Cor. 15:10). That is how a values-led life relates to ministry. This is because any action that derives from a great value is preferable to those actions that arise from a poor or unstated value.

[1]*anthonyingram.com/love-god-and-do-as-you-please/*

Chapter 18

Leading your church to be values-led

C reating a church that is values-led is very much what Jesus had to do with the Church He founded.

- He knew the end goal – a community committed to reaching the world;
- He knew about gathering the team and developing the inner circle;
- He knew He had to reframe their heart values – by patient teaching, sermons, parables, questions and experiences;
- He knew about lessons they could learn from outsiders like Roman centurions, a Syro-Phoenician mother, Samaritans, etc.;
- He knew about modelling His values so He could say, 'Follow Me – I am the way';
- He knew about empowering them and sending them out to practise.

It all took time. Sometimes there were steps forward followed by a few more in reverse. There were frustrations at how slow His disciples were to learn. He used appeals, rebukes, warnings, repetition, prayer, commendation, questions, illustrations, opportunities and defining moments – all focused on the one aim of growing His followers to run a values-led church. Did they grasp it perfectly? I don't think they did, but He so modelled and taught it that His followers brought into existence the greatest values-led change organisation on the planet – the Christian Church.

The primary task of the pastor today is to continue that goal of creating and sustaining the culture of a values-led community.

Peter S. Cohan argues that leaders of organisations must create a 'change team', and, 'To motivate the change team the CEO must generate enthusiasm for value leadership. To accomplish this the CEO must sponsor a seminar on value leadership designed to accomplish the following objectives:

- Define value leadership.
- Explain why value leadership is important.
- Describe the benefits of value leadership.
- Highlight the principles and activities that allow companies to apply value leadership.
- Present case studies of value leaders and peers.
- Conduct workshops that highlight the potential benefits of value leadership to the company.'

Value Leadership, page 255.

A 'change formula'

Some of those who describe the process involved in organisational change (e.g., Elaine Dickson) use this formula: (A+B+C)>D=Change. In this equation the components are defined as follows:

A: A significant level of dissatisfaction with some condition that presently exists within the organisation.

B: An awareness of an alternative, better condition that could exist.

C: The knowledge of the first step[s] to take in changing to the better condition.

D: The cost of making change.

Having said that, our real challenge is to describe a way (process) for this change to take place in the local church.

Here is a suggestion.

Start by getting to know the **thought leaders** of your church. These are the people that members look up to. Share your stories, dream with them and begin forming them into a values-led coalition of individuals who are eager for change. This is not to be achieved through high-pressure 'sales talk', but by almost casual discussion in which you share your thoughts and vision of a values-led community. This will begin creating a groundswell of support. It will help you to see the kind of questions and possible objections that you need to be ready to answer and persuade your members about later. It will also begin to create trust, admiration and appreciation of your leadership.

As you do this, emphasise both the importance and the urgency of the matter. Jesus stressed the urgency and importance of being value-led by saying that without values 'ye shall in no case enter into the kingdom of heaven' (Matt. 5:20, KJV). Without the sense of urgency '. . . the momentum for change will probably die far short of the finish line. People will find a thousand ingenious ways to withhold co-operation from a process that they sincerely think is unnecessary or wrongheaded.' (John Kotter, *Leading Change*, page 38.)

The next thing to do is call a meeting of your **elders**. Think of them as the preliminary change team that Cohen alludes to. You will now have moved from individuals or couples to a small group. Share your dream with them. Show them Bible examples of values. Give them some follow-up material to read about being values-led. Don't worry if they don't get it all – after three years Christ's disciples still had stuff to learn. Your aim is to gain their trust and loyalty. Again, with each of these groups it is vital to build trust and belief in the end goal. Without their passionate support and the credibility that comes with that you are trying to run 'an eighteen-wheeler truck propelled by a lawnmower engine' (J. Kotter, *Leading Change,* page 56).

Now it is time to take the matter to the **church board**. This is now your change team. Share the dream or vision with them, making sure that this meeting has ample time for the topic of values to be properly discussed. Do not be afraid to share the dream in bucketloads. Vision 'buckets' leak and need regular refilling. Get the next step in the process voted onto the next committee's agenda.

If, as a church, you and your leaders adopt a 'that will do' attitude, then the church will most likely remain a mediocre one. If you want to excel, however, then an 'only the best' attitude must prevail. I had the privilege of working with a master builder on a project in a certain country. His name was Robin, and he had a giant reputation for quality and was much sought-after for his work. He also had a compassion for the poor, and that is why he was on the project with us. We were building a home for a very poor man. Suddenly we began to run out of nails, and some helpers began pulling out nails from some old boards that we weren't using. When the first handful of these straightened nails got to Robin, he stopped and asked for new nails. We told him we had run out, and he paused as if struggling to find a solution before unhappily resigning himself to using the old nails. I asked him what was wrong, and he said, 'I have never used a nail twice before!' That is an example of how an 'only the best' attitude of a values-led person wins an outstanding reputation.

Begin talking about **biblical values** – how they can focus and benefit the church; how they can inspire, empower and retain our members, especially the youth; the need to be a church that 'exceeds' (Matt. 5:20); and how we can honour the values of our Father's Kingdom. Talk about the difference between values and the application of values, or the difference between values and local and cultural applications. Point out that churches that do not exceed the righteousness of the scribes and Pharisees *never* enter the Kingdom of Heaven (Matt. 5:20). Expose them to the value statements of admired churches and study together how those value statements could improve the culture of your church. Challenge each member to work on their own personal set of values, and be prepared for how the **Spirit of God** may inspire individuals on your board to move the process forwards.

When the time is right, use a **values assessment tool** and then share the results. You might ask each individual to do the assessment for him or herself first, and then do it together as a church. Try brainstorming an exhaustive list of values and then work together to select the top six or so as your own.

Now work on expressing those **values – clearly and succinctly**. Keeping them brief helps members to memorise them. After that let the board spell out the **implications of each value**. You can ask the question: 'If the church upholds this value, what will it look like?' Notice how, on the samples of value statements supplied (chapter 19), the implications of each value are worded in the subtext, but keep this to a short sentence or two.

While you are doing this, take note of **stories** that may arise out of the discussion. These may be either 'ouch' or 'wow' stories. Some of these may be stories about the founding of the church or about how various people became members ('wow' stories). They may also be stories of why some people left church ('ouch' stories). They are vital in embedding the values and their importance into the hearts of our members. Out of these may come a story that defines the essence of your church.

There is a school in Leicester, England, that I once visited that recovered from being a 'failed' institution to being an 'outstanding' one in every point on its annual government evaluation. When I first went there I noticed starfish woven into its carpets and engraved on each window. When I met the head teacher and asked about the starfish he told me this story. It was about a little girl walking along a beach after a storm had swept thousands of starfish onto the shore. The girl began picking them up and throwing them back into the sea. A passer-by told her that she was wasting her time – there were so many that her efforts would not make a difference. She responded by picking another one up and tossing it into the sea with this comment: 'It made a difference for that one!'

That story is known by every pupil and staff member of the school. It sums up their values. The school's annual government report states that 'The success of the school was really summed up by one Year 6 pupil who, quoting the school motto ("Each day you must make a difference"), said, "This tells us we must never give up – ever." '

After the church board has completed its value statement comes the really, really hard part – embedding those values into its leadership and membership culture. It needs to be taken to the **church business meeting** and on to every **member** repeatedly! Use every vehicle of communication available to your board – sermons, bulletins, newsletters, websites, calling cards, godly gossip. Share values success stories in Sabbath schools, youth meetings, Pathfinders and prayer meetings – at every possible opportunity. Moses would add, 'You shall teach them diligently to your children, and shall talk of them when you sit in your house, and when you walk by the way, and when you lie down, and when you rise.' (Deut. 6:7.)

Your **diaconate** is also very important. They are usually the first point of contact for members and visitors who attend your church. They are the face of the church. A series of sessions with the full team of the ladies and gentlemen who make up your diaconate is a must. They need to understand the values and demonstrate them to all who enter the doors of your church. A spirit of humble, loving and enthusiastic service to all should characterise them. The few words they speak may be worth more than all the words spoken in the sermon.

Organisations that know the value of service in winning the hearts and friendship and thereby the loyalty of their visitors, customers or members, make this skill paramount. They practise memorising the names of all they meet; they develop the skill of anticipating their needs; they know when to give the visitor space; they know how to press forward and when to hold back as they develop friendships with the visitors; they work out what is culturally relevant in the way they relate to people; how to give genuine compliments and how to develop the relationship at the visitor's pace.

One excellent practice that deacons can learn from Nordstrom's top salespeople is to carry a small book in which to jot down the names of all they meet and every detail they learn about them – their address, names of family members, their work, phone numbers, spouse's occupation, anniversary and birth dates, physical and spiritual needs, etc. They may also note down any likes and dislikes or stories about the family as these come to their knowledge. Of course this need not be all done at the first meeting and must be done only as the visitor volunteers the information. Then they work at memorising the information so that they can build the relationship. At the first meeting the deacon may only learn their names, but already what an impact the deacon can make as the person leaves after the meeting and hears, 'Goodbye Robert (or Raphaella), it has been a pleasure to meet you today. Do come again.' And how impressed they will be the next time they visit to be greeted by a genuine, 'Good morning, Robert – it's great to see you again. Welcome!' – and so the relationship grows.

And lastly, a values statement is an implicit **document of empowerment**. No one needs to ask permission of anyone to act in accord with the values of their church. In fact such acts are to be encouraged and applauded. Let me share a few examples of how some secular organisations do this with their employees.

Ritz-Carlton Hotel employees are each given a company credit card with permission to spend up to $2,000 per customer per day to give them outstanding service – one of the company's leading values. Employees do not need to ask their line managers for permission; they only need to return a receipt. They seldom use the facility, but the sense of empowerment and trust that each employee receives with the card embeds and reinforces the service value deeply into the Ritz-Carlton culture.

Southwest Airlines employees know that they will be supported in anything they do to make a flight fun for a traveller. At an airline desk the receptionist does not need to ask anyone for permission to change a flight ticket detail, and hosts and hostesses on their planes proactively find ways to make journeys a fun experience. For example, the story is told of a group of young students on a Southwest flight who request to help out on the plane. The hostess hands one of them the mike and they introduce themselves and then go about giving out the peanuts and talking to travellers. Everyone enjoyed the experience.

Both Ritz-Carlton and Southwest Airlines also expect their staff to live their company values when they are off duty. Their values are who they are!

For instance, Southwest Airlines enables, from its own resources, its employees to respond to needy neighbours both financially and with flight help. That empowerment allows employees to personally experience the joy of a real value from their neighbour as well as creating pride and loyalty in the values of their organisation.

Leading your church to be values-led is more than an intellectual thing. It must cascade down from the pastor to the church leaders, through the diaconate and into all the members – into their heads and hearts and then to their hands and feet. The values become who you are – your culture. Your number-one job as pastor is to be the chief 'culture officer', to guard the culture and make sure the church is what it says it is. And your second job is to be the chief communicator of the vision of your church.[1]

[1]See a statement by Sherry Stewart Deutschmann in a *New York Times* article entitled, 'My Previous Bosses Are Now My Customers', where she says, 'My No. 1 job is to be the chief culture officer, to guard the culture and make sure we are what we say. My No. 2 role is to be the visionary and communicate that vision to every member of the company.' *http://www.nytimes.com/2014/06/12/business/smallbusiness/my-previous-bosses-are-now-my-customers.html?smid=fb-nytimes&WT.z_sma=BU_MPB_20140612&bicmp=AD&bicmlukp=WT.mc_id&bicmst=1388552400000&bicmet=1420088400000&_r=5*

Chapter 19

Values assessment

Here is a values-assessment tool that can be used as is, or adapted by adding or removing values as needed to suit your circumstances.

Church ministry core values audit

Using the scale below, circle the number that best expresses the extent to which the following values are important to or characterise your church (actual values). Work your way through the list quickly, going with your first impression.

1	2	3	4
Not Important	Somewhat Important	Important	Most Important

1	Fairness: being treated impartially, without bias or prejudice	1 2 3 4
2	Family: people immediately related to one another by marriage or birth	1 2 3 4
3	Bible knowledge: a familiarity with the truth of the Scriptures	1 2 3 4
4	World missions: spreading the Gospel of Christ around the globe	1 2 3 4
5	Community: caring about and addressing the needs of others	1 2 3 4
6	Encouragement: giving hope to people who need it	1 2 3 4

7 Giving: providing a portion of one's finances to support the ministry — 1 2 3 4

8 Relationship: people getting along with one another — 1 2 3 4

9 Leadership: a person's ability to influence others to pursue God's mission for their organisation — 1 2 3 4

10 Cultural relevance: communicating truth in a way that people who aren't like us will understand — 1 2 3 4

11 Prayer: communicating with God — 1 2 3 4

12 Excellence: maintaining the highest of ministry standards that bring glory to God — 1 2 3 4

13 Evangelism: telling others the good news about Christ — 1 2 3 4

14 Team ministry: a group of people ministering together — 1 2 3 4

15 Creativity: coming up with new ideas and ways of doing ministry — 1 2 3 4

16 Worship: attributing worth to God — 1 2 3 4

17 Status quo: a preference for the way things are now — 1 2 3 4

18 Co-operation: the act of working together in the service of the Saviour — 1 2 3 4

19 Lost people: people who are non-Christians and may not attend church (the 'unchurched') — 1 2 3 4

20 Mobilised laity: Christians who are actively serving in the ministries of their church — 1 2 3 4

21 Tradition: the customary ways or the 'tried and true' — 1 2 3 4

22 Obedience: a willingness to do what God and others ask of a person — 1 2 3 4

23 Innovation: making changes that promote the ministry as it serves Christ — 1 2 3 4

24 Initiative: the willingness to take the first step or make the first move in a ministry situation — 1 2 3 4

25 Other values: — 1 2 3 4

Write down the values that you rated with a 3 or 4, then prioritise them. The first six are your church's core values. **(Taken from *Values-driven Leadership* by Aubrey Malphurs.)**

You can also use the same tool to help you decide what your individual core values are.

If the tool here doesn't suit you as an individual – sit down with a piece of paper and prayerfully jot down a short list of values (between 2 and 6). This is what I did when I created 'Llew's Constitution' (see the Introduction). You might take some suggestions from Malphurs' form. Then take some time – slower brains like mine might need lots of time – I took six months – to reflect, remove, refine and rank the values you end up with.

A church board can do the same. Each member fills out the above form, then you meet together and put all the names up on a board, then take time to collectively reflect, remove, refine and rank the values until you come up with what are or should be your church's core values. This should be done prayerfully and with as much time as all need.

Next comes the work of creating a value statement.

Chapter 20

What churches can learn from Ritz-Carlton hotels

The Ritz-Carlton Hotel organisation claims to uphold the highest quality of service of any organisation on earth. I wouldn't know – having never stayed in one of their exclusive hotels – but the stories and testimonials from their customers, as well as the profitability of the company, seem to support the claim.

Let me share what I think are the two main 'secrets' of their success, and then some comments on what I believe churches can learn from this company.

1. Define and refine

The company clearly defines what it values as good service. Then, after agreeing to those values, all of its employees strive to adhere to them and even refine them where possible. Staff members are employed on the basis of their ability to give good service. They go through an intensive series of interviews prior to employment, and then complete an annual course of training. Each employee understands that they are ladies and gentlemen serving ladies and gentlemen and that this is their company credo, namely:

The Credo
- The Ritz-Carlton is a place where the genuine care and comfort of our guests is our highest mission.
- We pledge to provide the finest personal service and facilities for our guests, who will always enjoy a warm, relaxed, yet refined ambience.
- The Ritz-Carlton experience enlivens the senses, instils well-being, and fulfils even the unexpressed wishes and needs of our guests.

Beyond the credo, there were (in 2006) 20 basics, which were expressed in 12 service values as follows:

Service Values
I am proud to be Ritz-Carlton
- I build strong relationships and create Ritz-Carlton guests for life.
- I am always responsive to the expressed and unexpressed wishes and needs of our guests.
- I am empowered to create unique, memorable, and personal experiences for our guests.
- I understand my role in achieving the Key Success factors, embracing Community Footprints, and creating the Ritz-Carlton mystique.
- I continuously seek opportunities to innovate and improve the Ritz-Carlton experience.
- I own and immediately resolve guest problems.
- I create a work environment of teamwork and lateral service so that the needs of our guests and each other are met.

- I have the opportunity to continuously learn and grow.
- I am involved in the planning of the work that affects me.
- I am proud of my professional appearance, language, and behaviour.
- I protect the privacy and security of our guests, my fellow employees, and the company's confidential information and assets.
- I am responsible for uncompromising levels of cleanliness and creating a safe and accident-free environment.

Beyond these basics and credo, each employee is encouraged to refine, given the individuality of each customer as well as their varying cultures, the application of the defined levels of service. Thus the credo and basics are not a set of defined rules, but rather a group of principles that are continually being refined.

2. Communicate the values

The values of Ritz-Carlton are embedded into the culture of the company in every way possible. Every employee carries the Company Credo Card with them. Each employee is empowered to spend up to $2,000 each day without reference to their supervisor in order to make sure that the needs of their customers are met. There are weekly line-ups when the credo and basics are repeated and the hotel manager shares stories from their hotels around the world of 'wow' service given by Ritz-Carlton employees. Every employee from the manager down is expected to evidence 'wow' service, not only to their customers, but to each other as well. This expectation includes the behaviour of an employee when they are not at work. Thus the whole culture of Ritz-Carlton is impregnated with their values.

Ritz-Carlton are 'fanatical' about instilling their values throughout their organisation because they believe that that is the secret of their present and future success.

Lessons for Adventist churches

While reading a study of the Ritz-Carlton culture here are some lessons that struck me.

- While Ritz-Carlton operates from the foundation of wealth (they would probably disagree with that statement), our churches are often composed of the less wealthy – as Paul wrote in 1 Corinthians 1:26 (NIV): 'Brothers and sisters, think of what you were when you were called. Not many of you were wise by human standards; not many were influential; not many were of noble birth.'

- Yet that should not be a reason why we cannot offer a warmth of service to each other and our visitors (our customers) that amounts to outstanding service. The service we can give should be modelled on the excellent hospitality that can be given (even in the poorest of homes) to family members and those we love, and not that which some might be tempted to offer to strangers. Jesus expected Kingdom people to exceed the actions of other people. There is no reason why outstanding hospitality-type service should not be a mark of our churches.

- We would do well to define what the good service that we want to offer in our churches should look like. We would have much to gain by the church leaders and the diaconate taking time to discuss some sort of 'credo' to define what kind of service we could give to our members and visitors. What might service that seeks to meet even the unexpressed needs of each person who comes to our churches look like? What could we do to make our visitors enjoy a 'wow' experience that creates loyalty and the desire to return?

- The Ritz-Carlton weekly 'line-ups' reminded me so much of Pathfinders, where at the start of each club we would repeat the Pathfinder law and pledge. Ritz-Carlton calls them credo and basics. But Ritz-Carlton takes them a step further – at each of their hotel line-ups the manager tells stories of employees and customers, gathered from their hotels worldwide, and uses these to inspire his employees to aspire with pride to the credo and basics themselves. Pathfinders might do well to learn from this, as might leaders of the diaconate and elders. We must first define our standards of service and then inspire our members to achieve them. And there is no better way of doing this than through stories that members can relate to and aspire to emulate. We aspire and do better by inspiration, rather than by bashing ourselves up.

- Empowered service. The $2,000-per-day provision to meet customer needs without reference to a supervisor is an amazing example of Ritz-Carlton empowerment. Our churches could never match that, but I wonder if they would even permit $20 to our deacons to meet visitor needs without reference to the treasurer. Could that be because we are so unclear of what our diaconate values are that we cannot risk trusting them with such empowerment? Ritz-Carlton believes that trusting and empowering frontline workers so unconditionally is what releases their greatness.

I believe that many, if not most, of our churches are places and organisations of potential greatness and beauty. My heart is saddened by reading of worldly organisations excelling in serving people and winning their loyalty and acclaim while comparing that to the poorly welcoming climates that our churches sometimes offer. I don't just believe in the church: I believe in the church in its beauty. That beauty could be greatly enhanced by defining our values clearly, then inspiring our members to achieve them with some focused training and stories of excellence. If as a community we strive to internalise those values and build a mutual trust, that can empower us to become that beautiful church. Oh, for the day when organisations like Ritz-Carlton ask the question, 'How come Adventist churches do it so well?'

Chapter 21

Examples of values-led statements

The following statements, or credos, as they are sometimes referred to, have been adapted from Aubrey Malphurs' book *Values-driven Leadership* and various websites. They are intended as examples to give the idea of the kind of statements your church can make. Don't simply copy them. Each value statement must grow out of your own context and result from prayerful interaction with the Word and the leading of the Spirit. It must be yours!

I suggest that a church working on a values statement simply browse through the samples below and then lay them aside and get on with designing their own unique expression of their core values.

Example 1
1. Love Jesus Christ
No one can love God for us. We must individually stay connected to Christ through an abiding relationship (John 15). Through the Word of God, prayer, personal worship, and obedience we can love God with heart, soul, mind, and strength.

2. Be connected through a small group

Community groups help us develop caring relationships with one another. In this small-group context we can get to know people, hold each other accountable, and offer newcomers a place to belong.

3. Build friendships with non-Christians

We can always be on the lookout for ways to reach out with the love of Christ to those who are teetering on the edge of a Christless eternity. By building relationships with non-Christians we may be able to communicate the life-changing message of salvation through Jesus Christ to them.

4. Participate in worship services

Weekly we gather together to celebrate God's goodness, be exposed to the Word of God, and catch up on family news. Our contemporary worship services provide ministry to believers and an open door to visitors and non-Christians in the community.

5. Pray regularly

When we pray we participate in the unseen spiritual world. Ministry is a battleground that needs to be constantly reinforced through prayer.

6. Give generously

Ministry takes money. Giving is one of the most tangible expressions of our faith. Believers are encouraged to give generously and sacrificially to the ministry of our church.

7. Serve faithfully

Christianity is not a spectator sport. Service is love in action. Through our God-given gifts and talents we find fulfilment and participate in the work of God in the world.

Example 2
1. A philosophy of grace

You cannot earn God's acceptance. He accepts you now and forever through faith in Jesus Christ. The church should not focus on guilt to motivate its members, but encourage them to live good lives from a motivation of love and thankfulness towards the Lord.

2. A Christian self-image

You can have a positive self-image, not because of who you are in yourself, but because of what God has done for you in Jesus Christ.

3. Biblical authority

You have an authoritative spiritual guide in the Bible, the Word of God. What the Bible teaches takes precedence over church traditions or human opinion.

4. Communicating Christ to the contemporary culture

You should be able to understand Christ and the Christian message because it should be communicated to you in a contemporary manner you can identify with and understand. The worship music in the church should be a type of music the contemporary person can relate to and understand.

5. Balanced Christianity

You need a balanced Christian experience that includes meaningful worship, life-related biblical teaching, significant relationships with other Christians, and the experience of serving others according to your gifts, abilities, and interests.

6. Every Christian is a minister

You, along with every other Christian, possess natural talents and spiritual gifts. As you release these talents and gifts for God to use, you will find more significance and purpose in your life.

7. Every Christian should be a 'world Christian'

You should be concerned to spread the Christian message to people of other cultures than your own, so they can share the same Christ who has helped you.

Example 3

1. A commitment to

creative forms and non-traditional methods of ministry.

2. A commitment to

Godly leadership.

3. A commitment to

encouraging all believers to use their spiritual gifts.

4. A commitment to

a Bible-centred teaching ministry.

5. A commitment to

cultivating a Christ-like and loving atmosphere within the body.

6. A commitment to

helping Christians develop a life of godliness in all areas of Christian living.

7. A commitment to

meeting the material needs of those in serious need, both within and outside our own body.

8. A commitment to

cultivating deep, abiding relationships within the body of Christ.

9. A commitment to

unity, love, and forgiveness among believers.

Example 4

1. A dedication to purpose

Our purpose is to lead people to salvation in Christ and growth in Christ-likeness.

2. A dedication to people
God works through people, and each person is unique and vital to God's plan.

3. A dedication to relationships
Building relationships is indispensable to spiritual health and spiritual growth.

4. A dedication to innovation
While our message is timeless, our methods must be adapted to those we're here to serve.

5. A dedication to quality
In everything we do, we give God only our best.

Example 5
1. We deeply value
the people of our town.

2. We deeply value
the truth and applicability of the Bible, God's Word to humankind.

3. We deeply value
our call to be relevant and involved.

4. We deeply value
personal authenticity and integrity.

5. We deeply value
excellence at every level.

6. We deeply value

the importance of healthy relationships, both with God and with one another.

Example 6

1. Scripture

A biblical message: We are committed to the clear and accurate communication of God's Word in a way that ministers grace and urges obedience (2 Tim. 3:16-17).

2. Creativity

A fresh approach: We are committed to forms of worship and ministry that will best capture and express what God is doing in our generation and culture (Luke 5:33-39).

3. Ministry

A team effort: We are committed to a team model for ministry and organisation that equips and empowers every family, member, and leader (Eph. 4:11-16).

This is only a brief selection of the many values-led statements that are available for your consideration. Internet searches will provide many more; however, it is important to stress that your members must engage in a discussion from which they extract a set of values that will be relevant to your own special circumstances. The process is important – not just the result!

Chapter 22

Listen

In this chapter we will provide practical advice on embedding the values into the befriending of visitors to your church and then into the skills you use when visiting in homes. Values must move off the Church's Statement into the heart and life of the church. As we saw in Chapter 18, that begins at the top with the minister, elders and board members, and then cascades to the diaconate and by example to every other member. The elders' and pastor's chief concern is the passionate championing of the values.

The deacon and the visitor

In the secular world, some businesses train their shop assistants to memorise their customers' names and other information about them. This translates from a feel-good factor into far greater customer loyalty, much more personal service and (of course) increasing sales for the company.

In the local church all would do well to recognise that these simple techniques can easily be adapted to developing relationships with visitors, which in turn contribute to friendships, community involvement, reciprocal loyalty and, ultimately, souls for the Kingdom.

Each deacon should carry a *pocket-size booklet* and pen or pencil to record the name of every visitor. Instead of a notebook you might want to use your mobile phone to record information. The deacon can also record other information that the visitors volunteer. Most people like being asked their names and don't mind a deacon saying, 'Let me write your name down to help me remember it.' Most people will be happy to think that you want to try and remember their name. They will be even more impressed if you greet them by name during the time of their visit, when they leave and if they return. To help memorisation, use their name as you talk with them – e.g. 'Robert, let me get you a programme.' 'Robert, it is such a pleasure to have you visit us today.' Then at every spare moment go over the names in your booklet and put faces to the names, pronouncing them as you do so. After everyone has gone home, take the time to review the names and faces again – you will be surprised how easily most of them come back to mind, and how thinking of them begins to bind your heart to ministering to them. Finally, in the evening take them one by one, name and face, to God in prayer.

It is very important that deacons be trained to be sensitive to how much information a visitor may wish to volunteer. Deacons must recognise that some people and cultures appear open, warm and affectionate while others may seem more reserved or distant. Respect that. Give them time to thaw. Be warm, but never pushy. If the only thing you learn at the first contact is their name – that is a huge step. Use that to show you care about them as a person – you know their name! Be conscious that some people do not like to be hugged, especially children. Let them lead in such matters. One young lady told me that she stopped going to a particular church simply because everyone kept hugging her!

Sentences such as the following should be standard and sincere among deacons:

- 'Welcome – is this your first time to our church?'
- 'I have seen you before but I don't yet know your name. Mine is . . .'
- 'John, let me get you a programme.'
- 'Ruth, the children's classes are through there and during our Bible study time we have three classes. I think you might enjoy being in the one that meets over there. And by the way, the toilets are over there.'
- 'David, would you like me to find seats for you? Where would you like to sit?' (Go and check that the seats are free before you take them there to save any embarrassment.)
- Deacons often vacate the foyer and allow the pastor to greet people as they leave, but deacons should look out for the new visitors and say goodbye. 'Sally, it was a pleasure to have you visit us today – do come again.'

The skill is to anticipate visitors' needs and concerns. The new visitor may be concerned about where their car is parked; about their children being cared for, or whether they will be scared of their new environment; about arriving late; where to sit; whether they need a hymnbook or Bible; and where the toilets are. The visitor may also be sight or hearing impaired, be confined to a wheelchair or walk with difficulty, all of which may require some assistance. Anything that you do to meet that need in a non-pushy way will create trust in you as they see your care for them. This will open the door for warmer relationships. Head deacons can sensitise their deacons to this through discussion and role-play.

The ministry of visitation

'Some of the reasons for visitation are: to become better acquainted with the membership; to strengthen new members and absentee members; to reclaim backsliders; to call on the sick and shut-ins; to identify and follow up on the needs of the elderly, disabled, widows, and single parents (such as house cleaning, yard work, meals, transportation, child care, home weather-proofing, and other improvements); to address family crises (such as spiritual problems, disaster, illness, domestic violence, bereavement, marital problems, financial problems, and children's behavioural problems); and to encourage faithfulness in matters of stewardship.'[1]

Expert visitation requires a loving, compassionate, serving heart; the wisdom God gives; and trained competence. Let the diaconate do some training in the skills outlined and become aware of ourselves and how we come across.

Firstly, develop a servant heart. The deacons need to love the 'sheep' assigned to their care. They will aspire to the humility of the Lord Jesus in serving His disciples and humanity in general. They will carry those members and families in their hearts, constantly bringing them to the Lord in prayer and asking Him to put love for them into their hearts.

Secondly, ask for wisdom. Before and during every visit they need to quietly claim the promise of wisdom given in James 1:5: '*If any of you lacks wisdom, let him ask God, who gives generously to all without reproach, and it will be given him.*'

Thirdly, learn the skills of visiting. Arrange for a competent person to give some training to the deacons in listening and counselling skills. In this training, teach your team how to observe confidentiality during and after their visits, remembering that loose talk can quickly undo all the good already achieved!

The author Parker Palmer uses the analogy of how to observe wild animals. If you charge into the jungle yelling for an animal to show itself – you will never see it. But if you sit quietly – listening and observing – it may appear when you least expect it and provide you with a spectacular experience.[2]

Your quiet and respectful **listening** is meant to allow the person being visited a chance to hear their own thoughts and be influenced by the Holy Spirit as to what they should do. Listening is not meant to be followed by advice from you. Try not to ask questions like:

- Don't you think you should see a therapist?
- Can't you see that the problem is . . . ?
- Have you read . . . ?
- Have you tried . . . ?

They are not really open, honest questions. They are actually advice in disguise and can shut people down.

Listen to what the Holy Spirit is saying about how Jesus can help the person. Get to know the stories of Jesus so that you can ask the Holy Spirit to impress you with the most appropriate one to tell or read. A story of Jesus that matches or applies to the person's experience can be a powerful influence on them.

If the person **appears open to help from someone else** and gives you permission to put them in touch with either your pastor or some other professional in the church, do so, but do not supply that person with any confidential information. Leave that for them to discuss when they meet.

Finally, **keep your visit as short as possible** without showing disrespect. The quality of your time listening rather than the quantity of your time counselling will create trust and make the visit a blessing.

Chapter 23

Choosing values-led officers

During our last general election I found it very difficult to decide who to vote for. It seemed that each party had policies that I liked and policies that I didn't like – strengths and weaknesses.

A similar situation often arises when a church chooses its officers for the coming year. Should our choices be based on competence, relationships, experience, theological bias, age, length of time as a member, friendship, or personal preference? I am sure that all of these have some bearing, but let me share some thoughts on choosing values-led officers.

There are several resources on church leadership that will discuss the three or four 'Cs' of leadership. I like the material on this topic in Bill Hybels' book, *Courageous Leadership*, pages 80-85.[1]

Essentially, the 3 Cs refer to character, competence and chemistry. By 'chemistry' he means the ability to relate well interpersonally. Character is clearly the most important quality that should be taken into account when choosing a leader – whether that leader is a board member, an elder or a member of the diaconate team. Sometimes we can find it difficult to define what we mean by good character. We should take into account traits such as honesty, faithfulness, humility, readiness to be submissive to the church, consistency and general disposition, etc. The values-led church, however, needs to add to that list an assessment of whether the person will passionately subscribe to the core values of the church. Some church leaders call this 'getting the right people on the bus'.

If you want the corporate culture of your church to reflect its core values, then the leaders that are chosen must be avid ambassadors of those core values. If a core value of your church is to welcome the stranger, it will be counter-productive to choose a very competent person to be one of your greeters if one of their leading values is that those attending church must conform to a strict dress code. Again, if your church's core values include reaching lost people, it is not good to choose a treasurer who is more concerned about saving money than saving people – or, for that matter, an organist or song leader who will insist on controlling *all* the music in a church that values diversity and inclusion.

What I am highlighting here is that core values are what should lead a church. The values should determine the vision, strategy, plans, and *the choice of leaders*, not the other way round. A values-led church, which is serious about its values, *chooses values-led leaders.*

Similarly, Conferences would do well to employ only workers whose values concur with the values the Conference is led by.

The second and third 'Cs' – competence and chemistry – may then be considered in choosing leaders. It goes without saying, and particularly if excellence is one of your church's values, that we should choose leaders of the best ability to do what they are asked to do. If excellence isn't a value, then I guess competence doesn't really matter. But keep in mind that competence can always be taught – values-led character can't!

Similarly, chemistry is an important factor in the leadership of the local church. Sometimes disagreeable (or incompetent) people can be given office or leadership roles because of tradition, or to placate some family or faction within the church. If placating people is a core value, then well and good. But to choose such a person, who will always be in conflict with the core values of the church, is unwise. It would be much more advantageous to choose someone within the DNA values or mindset of your church. Again, bear in mind that a values-led person can always be taught – character can't.

It would be better to choose a younger or inexperienced person if they already subscribe to your values or are eager to learn and embed those values. To find an older person who knows the culture and the history of the church and is passionate about its values is the ideal. Such a person not only can lead according to the values, but can be a mentor to the next generation of leaders.

Included in the competence and chemistry of a leader is the ability to know how to apply a core value to each situation. It is the difference between understanding what a value or principle is and knowing what an application is. The person who knows only the historical applications will, at some point, clash with the values of the dynamic church; whereas the values-led leader will always be on the lookout for how to do things even better, so as to honour the church's core values. Values-led leaders are open and creative. They seek and co-operate with the wisdom of the team. That does not mean that they are pawns, but that they are open to constructive criticism, eager to work together to fulfil the values of the church.

The leadership of Southwest Airlines provides an interesting example of the company's commitment to their values, and of how critical they believe this is to their organisation.

Their former CEO Herb Kelleher writes: 'We will hire someone with less experience, less education, and less expertise, than someone who has more of those things and has a rotten attitude. Because we can train people. We can teach people how to lead. We can teach people how to provide customer service. But we can't change their DNA.'[2]

In their hiring process, they screen early for attitudes towards the company values, one of which is a 'fun' attitude to customers. The story is told of some six Air Force pilots who applied for employment with Southwest. There was no question of the competence of each pilot. Prior to an interview they were each asked to go into a cubicle and put on the clothes that were hung there. These included short trousers and brightly coloured casual shirts. Three of the pilots, used to the disciplined neatness and appearance of the Air Force, refused to put the clothes on. They were politely told that their interview was over. Southwest would not employ a person with a negative attitude to their core value of fun.

On another occasion an applying pilot was asked to go to a particular Southwest desk and arrangements would be made for them to fly to their interview. Apparently the pilot was impatient and discourteous to the Southwest desk clerk. The clerk reported the travel arrangements to the interviewing office and also the rudeness of the pilot. The pilot shortly thereafter received a call to say that the interview was cancelled and that Southwest could not employ a person who was impolite to a possible future colleague. The pilot had run up against a value that would not be compromised.

The values-led church should take its values very seriously. If a person being considered for office does not subscribe to even one of the values, it would be better to slow down any nomination and re-evaluate the suitability of the person to the office. Better to struggle through a year without a leader or to find another way of providing that leadership than to discover partway through a term of office that the wrong person has got on the 'bus' and that the culture of the church and its core values are at risk.

[1]Bill Hybels: *Courageous Leadership*, Zondervan, 2002, pp. 80-85.
[2]*http://www.logomaker.com/blog/2012/05/21/9-inspirational-quotes-on-business-by-herb-kelleher/*

Chapter 24

When the team seems to be falling apart

T he story of Elijah fleeing from Jezebel so soon after his stunning courage and victory over the prophets of Baal is a classic story of everything going splendidly – then suddenly going pear-shaped.

We tend to see any hopes or changes that we wish for our churches as following a steadily upward trajectory – possibly even the expectation of a miraculous change following an inspired sermon – but in reality that rarely happens. More likely it feels like we are driving a car where the timing is out or one of the pistons is not firing. Occasionally it just stops. And our plans for the church, which felt like a fine car that we expected great things of, feel like a lemon. Then we take it personally and go through the Elijah thing, and then fail to persevere and trust that our God who knows best often takes the long route.

Values do not suddenly perfect people and organisations. It is not difficult to find stories of acts within values-led organisations, secular and Christian, that, through greed, the lust for power, abuse of others, etc, have led to corporate and individual betrayal of their core values. Great organisations like Southwest and Nordstrom as well as churches are only too well aware of this. The early church had Peter with his religious and cultural bigotry to deal with (Acts 10); Ananias and Sapphira, who succumbed to greed (Acts 5); deserters like Demas (2 Tim. 4:10); false brethren (Gal. 2:4); and hypocritical and sexually immoral members (1 Cor. 5:1).

If presented graphically, the experience of each church is unlikely to be a steadily ascending straight line. It is most likely to be a squiggly line with a number of dips and high points, but it will be an ascending line that describes the reality of a community striving to do better and to rise above the mediocrity of the world around them. Why? Because they know and aspire to the values of the 'more excellent way' (1 Cor. 12:31).

This is true of both organisations and individuals. A work colleague of mine shared with me recently about his aspirations to embed a 'grace' value into his life. His experience was that of daily falling short and an increasing recognition of his 'self-bentness', but also of being inspired by the example of Christ and a growing desire to walk closer to Him and to imitate Him more and more.

My comment in response was that being values-led is the work of becoming more and more like Christ, and this is a long-term project – that of a lifetime. My thoughts came from a wise pen that wrote: 'Sanctification is not the work of a moment, an hour, a day, but of a lifetime. It is not gained by a happy flight of feeling, but is the result of constantly dying to sin, and constantly living for Christ. Wrongs cannot be righted nor reformations wrought in the character by feeble, intermittent efforts. It is only by long, persevering effort, sore discipline, and stern conflict, that we shall overcome. We know not one day how strong will be our conflict the next. So long as Satan reigns, we shall have self to subdue, besetting sins to overcome; so long as life shall last, there will be no stopping place, no point which we can reach and say, I have fully attained. Sanctification is the result of lifelong obedience.' (Ellen G. White, *Acts of the Apostles*, page 560.)

Churches that commit to being values-led will walk the same path, but they can have the advantage of being places where, if one stumbles, they will be surrounded by fellow travellers who understand the common struggle and will provide the support and care that are needed to press on to the values they hold in common and in their unity.

Greater leaders than we are will testify that the road of leadership is not always a shortcut. Moses would probably tell us that it took approximately 39 years and 11 months longer than he imagined, to get the church he led to shift location. And Jesus seemed to struggle with foolish, 'slow of heart' believers even after three and a half years (Luke 24:25).

Just three or four days before walking the Emmaus road (Luke 24) He had gathered His disciples to share a last meal with Him before His trial and the cross. The mindsets and agendas in that room must have made it feel like many a modern-day board meeting.

In spite of repeated sermons, private talks, stories and experiences to reveal His core values and His commitment to the cross, none understood the mind of the Leader or grasped His understanding of the events before Him. The 'treasurer' knew what needed to be done and how economics would bring about the desired end. Two of the 'directors' were openly campaigning for the head elder's office. They had even brought in an elder statesman – Jesus held a soft spot for mothers – to present the emotional argument for their case. The rest were playing politics. Didn't they all have every right to aim for the top offices? One begins to wonder if they had begun counting up the number of contacts, studies and baptisms that could be credited to themselves. Jesus, the CEO of His church and indeed of the universe, and with His standing soon to be confirmed by Heaven itself, must have looked about Him in despair. Seated near Him was one who would, that very night, sell Him for a mere 30 pieces of silver; a little further along was one who would betray Him with curses; and all would desert Him. If ever the dream team was falling apart, this was it. And time was not on His side. He knew He was about to leave. What does the leader do when the team seems to be falling apart?

John records the action.

He 'rose from supper. He laid aside his outer garments, and taking a towel, tied it around his waist. Then he poured water into a basin and began to wash the disciples' feet and to wipe them with the towel that was wrapped around him.' (John 13:4-5.)

The Leader never gives up on His values. He is true to His nature. He is always values-led.

Chapter 25

The power of a value

For most people, beatings, stonings, shipwrecks, hunger, thirst, deprivation and discouraging events and much more would destroy their motivation to continue on in a task or career. Not the apostle Paul! After being stoned and left for dead outside a city wall one would have expected him to take at least some weeks off for recuperation from his injuries – which are likely to have included lacerated skin, a cracked skull and broken ribs. Not Paul – the account in Acts 14 records him travelling onwards the next day to continue his ministry in another city.

What drove Paul? What was his motivation?

It is an 'aside' that gives us a glimpse into the value that was the dynamic in Paul's life. He had written a number of chapters outlining the struggles and giving advice to the church in Corinth, with its divisions over gifts, roles, and behaviour. Then he showed them a better way, the way of love, in the magnificent chapter of 1 Corinthians 13. There follows in the next chapter an explanation of how order is built on relational love. Then, in chapter 15, he brings them back to the most basic of their beliefs – the resurrection of Christ. In doing so he, almost as an aside, draws the curtain back on the motivational drives of his heart. He writes: 'Last of all, as to one untimely born, he appeared also to me. For I am the least of the apostles, unworthy to be called an apostle, because I persecuted the church of God. But by the grace of God I am what I am, and his grace toward me was not in vain. On the contrary, I worked harder than any of them, though it was not I, but the grace of God that is with me.' (1 Cor. 15:8-10.)

What drove him to work 'harder than any of them'? The story of 'grace'.

Notice that the apostle does not tell us that it was the truth – or even the thrill of the resurrection – that drove him. It is a relationship with the love or grace of God that created or is behind that truth, that motivates him. Paul experiences the grace of God, and that grace relationship empowers him. In working out what our values are we must not make the mistake of replacing truth for the motivation that derives from a personal encounter and relationship with the character of God. In the book *Encouragement: The Key to Caring*, page 84, authors Crabb and Allender write that '... the presentation of truth without a discerning awareness of people's hunger for relationship and identity may do nothing more than crowd people into a legalistic box. Behaviour may change, but the inward reality will likely be pressured conformity with no experience of the liberty and love of Christ. Relationship without truth leads to shallow sentimentality. Truth without relationship generates pressure, then friction, and eventually disillusionment or pride.'

Ellen White comments on the relationship between truth and grace thus: '*It is no real evidence that one is a Christian because his emotions are stirred, or his spirit aroused, by the presentation of truth.* The question is, Are you growing up into Christ, your living head? Is the grace of Christ manifested in your life? God gives His grace to men, that they may desire more of His grace. God's grace is ever working upon the human heart; and when it is received, the evidence of its reception will appear in the life and character of the recipient, for spiritual life will be seen developing from within. *The grace of Christ in the heart will always promote spiritual life,* and spiritual advancement will be made. We each need a personal Saviour, or we shall perish in our sins. Let the question be asked of our souls, Am I growing up into Christ, my living head? Am I gaining advanced knowledge of God, and of Jesus Christ, whom He hath sent?" *Address to Ministers,* p. 18.

Again in *The Messenger* of 6 July, 1893, page 1, Ellen White writes, 'The grace of Christ alone could change the heart of stone to a heart of flesh, make it alive unto God, and transform the character, so that a degraded child of sin might become a child of God, an heir of heaven.'

Again: 'Nothing reaches so fully down to the deepest motives of conduct as a sense of the pardoning love of Christ.' *The Desire of Ages*, page 493.

Jesus, in His parable of the four soils, points out that it is not the *seed* or its joyful reception that gives staying power to the believer but rather the *root* that is the staying power of the believer. And surely that root is being anchored into the gracious person of God.

How does that work? Let Paul explain. In 1 Corinthians 15 verses 9 and 10 he tells us that he was in effect an unwanted abortion, the great enemy of the church, its persecutor – why would any of the church want to associate with him? Yet, God, by grace – unexpected, undeserved – and grace alone, made him an apostle. It is this experience of the core value of God's character that picks Paul up each day, even from an attempted stony execution, to meet the next challenge.

This discovery of 'our value' in the eyes of the greatest Person of the Universe is the key to Paul's existence and mission. Neil Ormerod, in his book, *Grace and Disgrace*, explains it thus: 'In a sense we may think of our self-esteem as our basic question to the cosmos – am I worthwhile? Is my existence meaningful? My life's quest is to find an answer to this question, an answer which I seek from parents, from friends and lovers, through careers and financial success, through a happy and rich family life. Ultimately I seek the answer from God, who is the very source of my existence. All the answers I hear, or think I hear, all the truth and lies from all these sources leave an almost indelible mark on my character, shaping me, forming me, for better or worse. All the evidence indicates that the most significant source is my parents, the proximate cause of my being. If my parents love and nurture me then I develop a bedrock of self-esteem which lasts a lifetime. If my parents, the people who are the source of my life, neglect me, if I am not of value to them then the damage done can be irreparable in human terms. If those who made me do not love me, then I must at heart be unlovable! Experience shows how even children who suffer the most serious neglect from their parents will seek them out in some desperate hope of a kind word or some grudging affirmation.

'Where self-esteem has been so damaged there are a variety of strategies which can be developed to bolster it. Some seek to bolster it through a single-minded commitment to a career. Some seek to bolster it by putting other people down – "I must be good because I'm so much better than them!" Such self-righteousness, particularly religious self-righteousness, is a common problem. The parable of the Pharisee and the publican is a classic example (see Luke 18:9-14). Some try to bolster their self-esteem by seeking public office that carries prestige, such as priesthood or political office. All such strategies are short-term solutions. They work for a while, but soon the demon within requires a greater satisfaction. Then such strategies can easily fall over into despair: "I really am worthless after all. . . ." To counter such a grim scenario we all need an affirmation that goes right to the heart of the matter, a truly unconditional love, something that affirms our existence without qualification, without reserve. Such is the solution offered by grace.'

How did it affect Paul? In verse 10 he tells us that he worked harder than them all. But, lest we think he is boasting, he tells us that this is not because of himself, but rather the driving value of 'grace' that ordered his actions and life. Did the prodigal son work harder when he came home than he did before he left home? Surely he did. That is the effect of a relationship with the gracious Father.

How does grace do that? Paul is telling us that in the company of grace his enthusiasm for his vision – and the gifts to achieve it – were continually being enthused and equipped. Just as the grace of God drove Jesus Christ to the hardship of the cross and then to the resurrection, so Paul was driven by that inspiring grace.

That's what a value – experienced, understood and then embedded into one's own life – does.

Jesus commanded that His church be a values-led church. 'Love one another,' He instructed them (John 13:34). That is how the world would get to know that we are discipled followers of His. Here in 1 Corinthians 15 the apostle Paul gives an insight into his personal values-led life after giving a description of what that grace and love look like in 1 Corinthians 13. Imagine what such a values-led church would look like.

Chapter 26

Would you stone a 'Sabbath breaker'?

This reflection is based on the story of Jesus healing the man with the withered hand in Mark 3:1-6. The incident impacts so strongly on the Pharisees that the story ends with them making plans to kill Jesus.

It raises this question: Would you or I kill a 'Sabbath breaker'? Who, in this case, happens to be the Lord of the Sabbath!

This story might help us understand what is happening in the text. It is about an old man with a perfect lawn, who became fed up with a young lad who had walked across his perfect lawn a number of times over a period of years. The old man repeatedly told him not to but the lad kept on doing it, until one day as the youth crossed the lawn the old man picked up his shotgun, walked out and shot him dead!*

This story bears some parallels to our passage, especially when we take the time to read the second chapter of Mark as background. For it contains a number of stories in which Jesus, as it were, crosses the 'perfect lawn' belonging to the Pharisees and rabbis of His day.

The first is when four friends lower their paralysed companion through the roof of the house where Jesus is preaching (Mark 2:1-12). Some commentators suggest that the Pharisees knew this man and believed that his condition was the deserved result of his own sins: which simply means that when Jesus assured him of forgiveness and healed him, it would have been seen as a direct affront to both their theology and personal dignity. *Jesus was walking across their lawn.*

Mark's second story (Mark 2:13-17), the one of Jesus calling Matthew Levi to become a disciple, would similarly have been a direct affront to these religious leaders. Mark notes that Levi is sitting at his tax booth, busy practising his treacherous and wicked work, when Jesus calls him. In the eyes of these religious leaders no self-respecting, godly person would do such a thing. Jesus had no business eating with publicans (tax collectors) and such despicable sinners. Jesus' action is, again, an affront again to their values and thinking. *Jesus was walking across their lawn, again.*

The next story is found in Mark 2:18-22. In the thinking of the religious people of that day the fasting of John's disciples and that of the Pharisees gave them a higher spiritual ranking. In this setting Jesus and His disciples are trailing a very distant third in the spirituality ratings; even His cousin is doing better! Then, to make things even worse, Jesus says that to experience joy in His presence is more important than fasting, which is another affront to their system of how you earn 'Brownie points' with God. *Jesus was trespassing on that lawn again!*

The fourth story (Mark 2:23-28) brings us much closer to those religious authorities' self-appropriated area of responsibility – Sabbath keeping. When challenged about why His disciples ate corn while they walked through the fields on Sabbath, Jesus' response was a direct affront to the Pharisees and their associates. He refers to the conduct of

David in justifying the feeding of his soldiers with the showbread (1 Samuel 21:1-9), and endorses it.

This how Mark records the incident: 'He answered, *"Have you never read what David did when he and his companions were hungry and in need? In the days of Abiathar the high priest, he entered the house of God and ate the consecrated bread, which is lawful only for priests to eat. And he also gave some to his companions.'* (Mark 2:25-26, NIV.)

Jesus was clearly delivering a hammer blow to their rabbinical rules about Sabbath keeping, and they didn't like it one bit. *Jesus was walking over their lawn once again!*

Then we come to the synagogue story of Mark 3:1-6, where Jesus becomes guilty of the greatest sacrilege so far – healing a man in the synagogue on the Sabbath.** He has walked across 'their lawn' once too often and now (my paraphrase) 'the Pharisees went out and began to plot with the Herodians on how they might obtain a shotgun and kill Jesus.'

Why did the old man shoot the youth?

People get angry when a perceived reality or a core value – something that is theirs and defines them – is threatened. The old man saw his lawn as the symbol of his personal dignity and worth, while the youth's persistent action of walking across the manicured lawn became a direct affront to that personal worth. His frustration led to anger, which in turn led to the shotgun. A team of Yale University scholars in a study back in 1939 concluded that 'aggression is always the consequence of frustration.' (Louis Raths in *Meeting the Needs of Children*, Educator's International Press, 1998, page 18.)

Why were the Jews angry?

They were angry because Jesus was persistently trampling on what gave them their value before God. If their meticulous Sabbath keeping, fasting, and abhorrence of despicable, wilful sinners didn't give them personal value before God, what were they doing those things for?

This may appear trivial, but it isn't. If I come to church with my tie and suit on, isn't God pleased? And if that is so, isn't the converse also true – that He frowns on scruffy people without suits and ties! But then if the 'sinner' keeps being blessed, as Jesus seems to be doing in all the above stories, then what is the Pharisees' 'righteousness' for? Jesus is making the things that the Pharisees strive for appear of little value.

Is Jesus against religious practices such as careful Sabbath keeping, fasting and avoiding evil? Of course not, but Jesus is against the attitude of the Pharisees in which they were very particular about minor religious and worship practices that focused on themselves, while judging and treating other people with disdain.

The Pharisees' values clustered around themselves, which is contrary to God's core values of other-centredness and grace. Thus they distanced themselves from the values of the Kingdom of Heaven and ended up harbouring murderous intentions towards their King.

Would you stone a 'Sabbath breaker'?

The answer depends on what gives you value. If it is your lawn (like the old man in our story); your possessions (like the rich young ruler); your greed for the vineyard (like the tenants in the vineyard parable [Matt. 21:33-40]); your desire to be honoured (like the older brother in the parable of the prodigal son); the desire to justify yourself (like the lawyer in Luke 10:29); or your approval of the punishment of all who disagree with you (like Saul in Acts 8:1-3), then beware. For may I humbly submit to you that you are not being led by the values of the Spirit of God, and that you would stone the Sabbath breaker – even if He be the Lord of the Sabbath Himself!

*http://www.cbsnews.com/news/blood-spilled-over-mans-perfect-lawn/

**'The rabbis had waited anxiously to see what disposition Christ would make of this case. They recollected how the man had appealed to them for help, and they had refused him hope or sympathy. Not satisfied with this, they had declared that he was suffering the curse of God for his sins. These things came fresh to their minds when they saw the sick man before them. They marked the interest with which all were watching the scene, and they felt a terrible fear of losing their own influence over the people.' *Desire of Ages*, page 268

Chapter 27

Could Jesus have done it differently?

I refer the reader to the same passage we looked at in the previous chapter, namely Mark 3:1-6, and pose this question: Why didn't Jesus make an appointment to heal the man at another time and place, rather than cause all this anger and confrontation on the Sabbath in a church?

Jesus could have, for the sake of peace, told the man with the withered hand that at sunset his hand would automatically heal. Alternatively, He could have asked the man to meet him the next day for healing, or at least taken him outside the synagogue, so as not to offend the religious leaders, and healed him.

Why didn't Jesus do that?

I would submit that Jesus couldn't take any of those options.

Jesus is angry too! 'Then Jesus asked them, "Which is lawful on the Sabbath: to do good or to do evil, to save life or to kill?" But they remained silent. He looked around at them in anger and, deeply distressed at their stubborn hearts, said to the man, "Stretch out your hand." He stretched it out, and his hand was completely restored. Then the Pharisees went out and began to plot with the Herodians how they might kill Jesus.' (Mark 3:4-6, NIV.)

Jesus' anger is illustrated by the stories of Him casting the money changers out of the Temple. The four accounts are found in Matthew 21:12-13; Mark 11:15-18; Luke 19:45-46; and John 2:13-17. It is interesting to read through those passages and find that the word 'anger' is not used. The word 'zeal' is used in John's account, but not the word 'anger'.

Here in the synagogue incident of Mark 3:1-6, however, we are told that Jesus looks around at them with 'anger'. The Greek word used for looking around is περιβλεψάμενος, from which you get the sense of a focused and deliberate, searching look. Mark uses the same word in Mark 11:11 and adds that Jesus looked at 'everything'. The careful Dr Luke, in his account of the synagogue incident in Luke 6:10, tells us that Jesus looked round at them 'all' before speaking. And the word to describe His look that day is 'anger'!

The Greek word 'anger' here is used only once of Jesus. It is the word ὀργῆς. It is the same word used by John in Revelation to describe what is in God's cup of final wrath (Rev. 14:10): 'he also will drink the wine of God's wrath, poured full strength into the cup of his anger.' It is striking to note that the one record of Jesus' anger shows it focused at His own people. Jesus is so focused on what He sees as vitally important that He is not going to shift this matter to another time or place. This is a 'hill to die on'!

Before we explore why, please notice that though both Jesus and the Pharisees are angry, the anger of the church leaders results in murder. Theirs is an anger that kills, while an added word gives us a completely different perspective on the nature of Jesus' anger. The text says that Jesus' look of anger was accompanied by grief at their hardness of heart (Mark 3:5). 'He looked around at them in anger and, **deeply distressed at their stubborn hearts**, said to the man,

"Stretch out your hand." He stretched it out, and his hand was completely restored.' (Mark 3:5, NIV, emphasis supplied.)

Here the Greek word for this grief is συλλυπούμενος – a word that is used only once in the New Testament – how careful the writers are to make sure we understand the uniqueness of the heart of Jesus. The word means 'grieving with someone'. He is angry, but this anger is accompanied by a grief or compassion for His people, not a desire to kill.

I recall an incident in my home when I saw my two boys, quite young at the time, playing with some neighbourhood friends just 50 or so metres from our home. But they were attacking a small tree in the park. I ran to the door and shouted at them. The other boys ran off but I commanded my boys home and set about telling them off strongly. I was angry with them. One of them then turned to me and, through his tears, said, 'But Daddy, the other boys were doing it too – why are only we getting the telling off?' Compassion welled up in me and I drew them close and tried to explain that it was because I loved them dearly. Here Jesus is driven by an 'angry' love of which mine was only a weak shadow.

Let us go over the four stories of Mark 2:1-28 and this time note, not the Pharisees' values, but Jesus' values.

In the first story, of the man who comes down through the roof, notice Jesus' first action. It is to tell the man that he is forgiven. He does not ask the man his name, or what he wants, as with blind Bartimaeus (Mark 10:51). Jesus does not enter into a dialogue to make certain the man understands any basis of the coming healing. He simply offers the man forgiveness, and that to a man who has probably caused his own condition. **It is the nature of the Son of Man to**

dispense forgiveness freely.

In the next story, Levi – just as he is, sitting at his tax booth, apparently conducting his business – is invited to follow Jesus. That is the nature of our Jesus. It is how you and I entered His Kingdom. Then we find Jesus at Matthew's house, associating with those whom religious people usually avoid. This reveals that His heart is that of a spiritual doctor committed to bringing healing to sinful hearts. He holds to a standard that soars above any Hippocratic oath. What is that standard or core value? In Matthew's account of the story, Jesus instructs them clearly: 'Go and learn what this means: "I desire mercy, and not sacrifice" ' (Matt. 9:13). **Mercy comes first in the heart of Jesus. It always has.**

To the question about fasting we find Him delighting in a joyful love relationship with His people. It is a love relationship wherein the bridegroom has a love so deep that He commits Himself to being 'taken away'. Here is an expression of violence against Him that commentators see as the first indicator of the coming cross. His departure is not to be voluntary, but violent. The LXX of Isaiah 53:8 uses the same verb to indicate that 'hostile oppression and judicial persecution were the circumstances out of which He was carried away by death.' (Keil and Delitzsch, *Commentary on the Old Testament*, on Isaiah 53:8.) Here is a Bridegroom that commits Himself to death for a bride before the wedding takes place. **How deeply embedded in Christ is the nature of this love.**

In the fourth story, in the grainfield, Jesus refers to the kindness of the great King David and his principle or value that overrides even that 'which it is not lawful for any but the priests to eat'. The implication is that if David can do that, can the Son of Man, one greater than David, greater than the Temple (see Matt. 12:6) and the Lord of the Sabbath, not act out of His mercy towards people?

The above stories illustrate powerfully that *mercy*, *grace*, and *abounding steadfast love* (compare Exodus 34:6-7) form the core description of God's nature and therefore of Jesus' nature too. It always has been and is an often-repeated message of the Old Testament prophets to Israel – see, for instance, Isaiah 1:12-17 and Micah 6:7-8. As the lyrics of a modern song say: 'God loves people more than anything' – Pharisees included!

Mercy towards people is the driving passion and core value of Jesus' heart. It is His very nature!

Now let us answer our question: Why didn't Jesus make an after-Sabbath appointment with the man to heal his hand?

When we ask that question we are asking Him to change His nature – His core value – to put an act of worship before that of mercy. We will have reversed what He wants us to learn. He can't – and, praise God, He can't and won't.

Why? Because I need His nature to be that of mercy and grace, for it is the only hope of my salvation and the source of my personal value. If my name comes up in the judgement – at any time – my earnest prayer is, 'Lord Jesus, please don't have anything more important to do than to have mercy on one such as me.'

I am valued because He values me – and you, and all the tax collectors, the prodigals, the prostitutes and the sinners! We are valued far more than we can or ever will understand.

These beautiful stanzas from the song 'Above all powers' say it all:

Crucified
Laid behind the stone

You lived to die
Rejected and alone

Like a rose trampled on the ground
You took the fall
And thought of me
Above all

Jesus never puts Sabbath keeping or worship or dress code or fasting or feasting or anything above our need for His mercy and grace. These are values He will not compromise.

A TV commercial by the hotel chain Shangri-La* is worth watching to note two things: firstly, their chain's core value, 'To embrace a stranger as one's own'; and secondly, the advert's claim about that value: 'It's in our nature.'

The advert is an echo of Jesus' core value of mercy to all. To embrace the stranger as one's own well describes the core value of Jesus. We see it over and over through His life – in His touching the leper; stopping in a crowd to talk to a woman who touches the hem of His garment; embracing children; asking for a drink from a Samaritan woman; answering the requests of a pagan centurion and a Syro-Phoenician woman. We see it clearly taught in the picture He paints of a father running to embrace a prodigal son.

Why does Jesus do these things? It is in His nature. Mercy describes His behaviour and His being. Thus it was not possible for Him to pass the man with the withered hand or delay his healing!

*https://www.youtube.com/watch?v=wZeSOUn3jwk